Lacy Sunsh

Fairy Enchantresses

Illustrated by
Heather Valentin

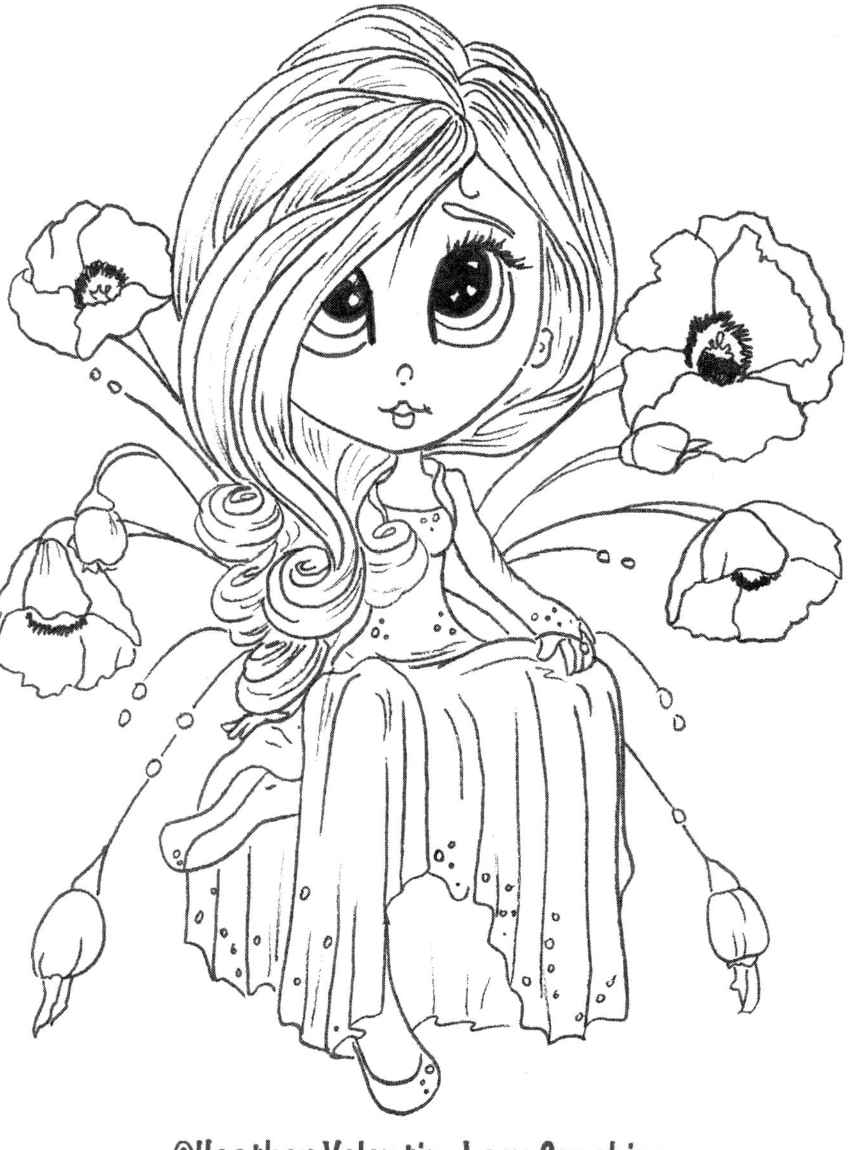

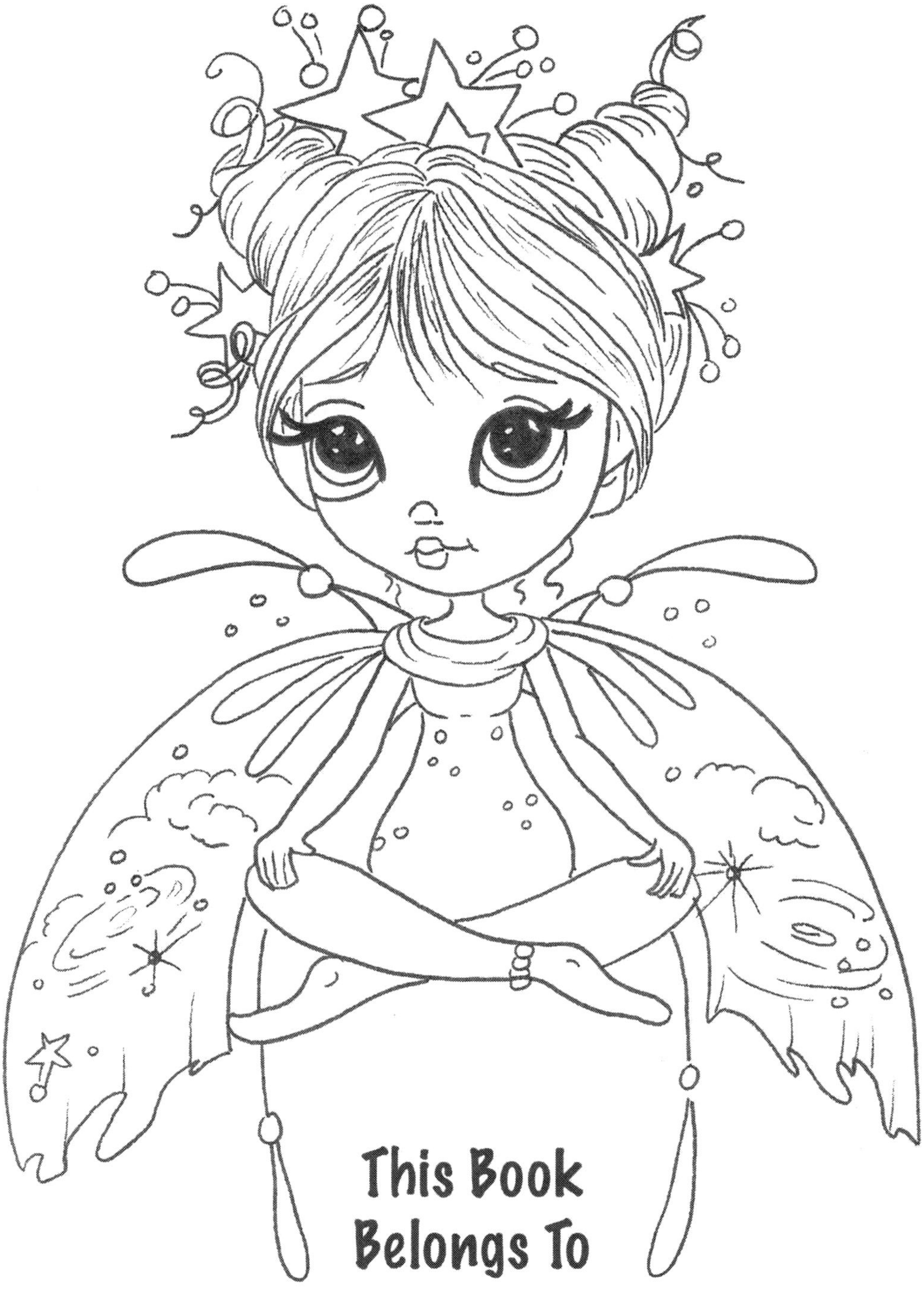

This Book
Belongs To

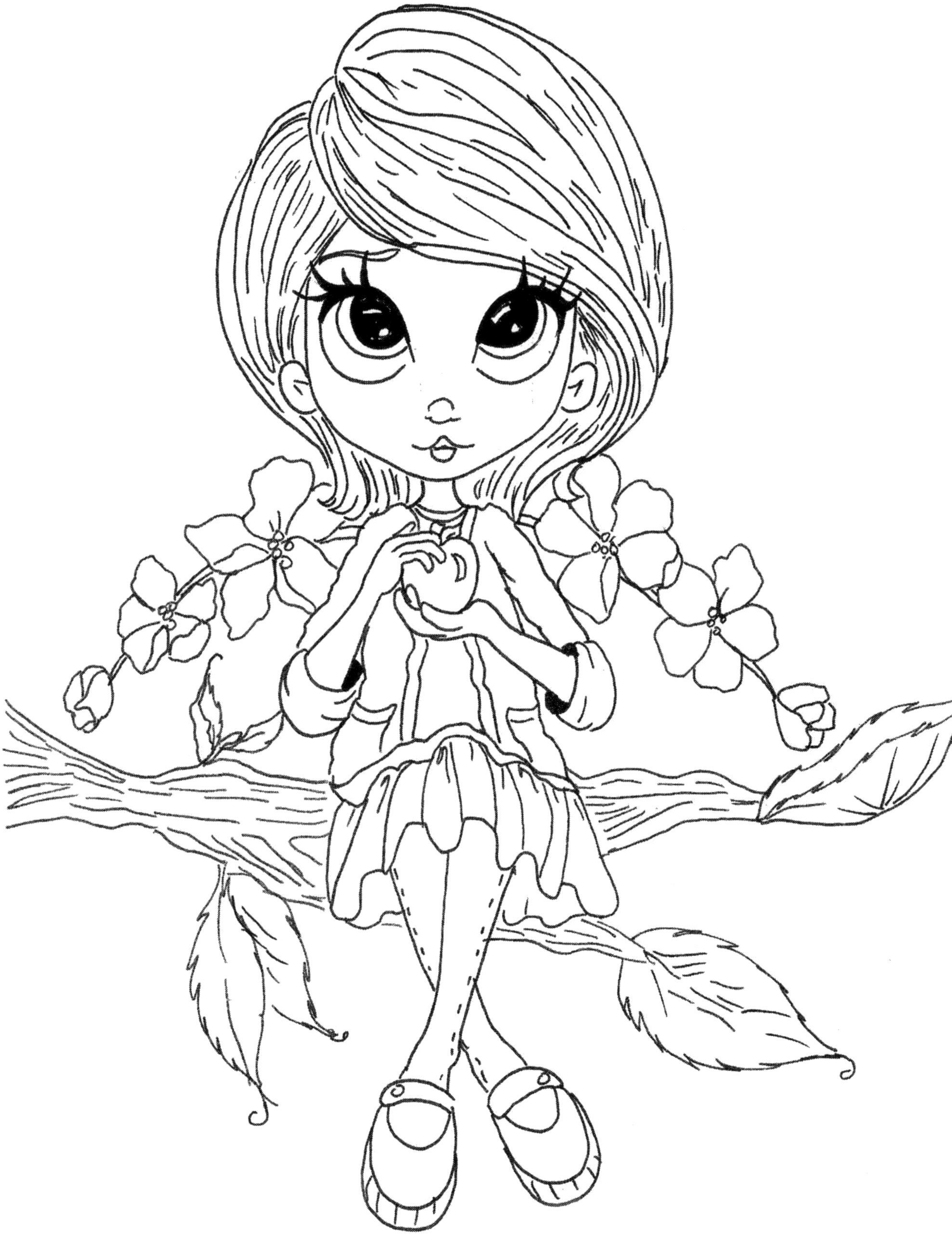

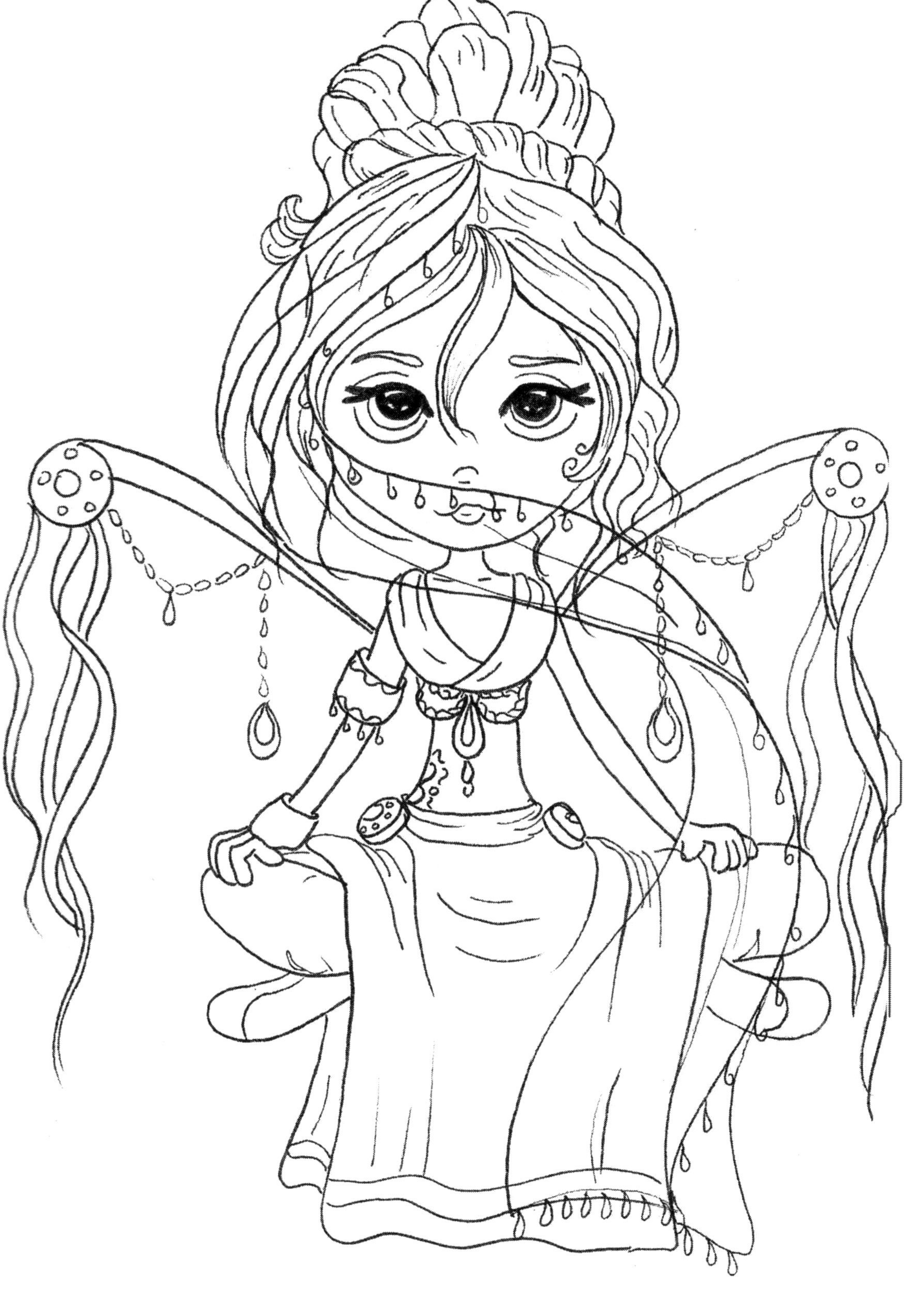

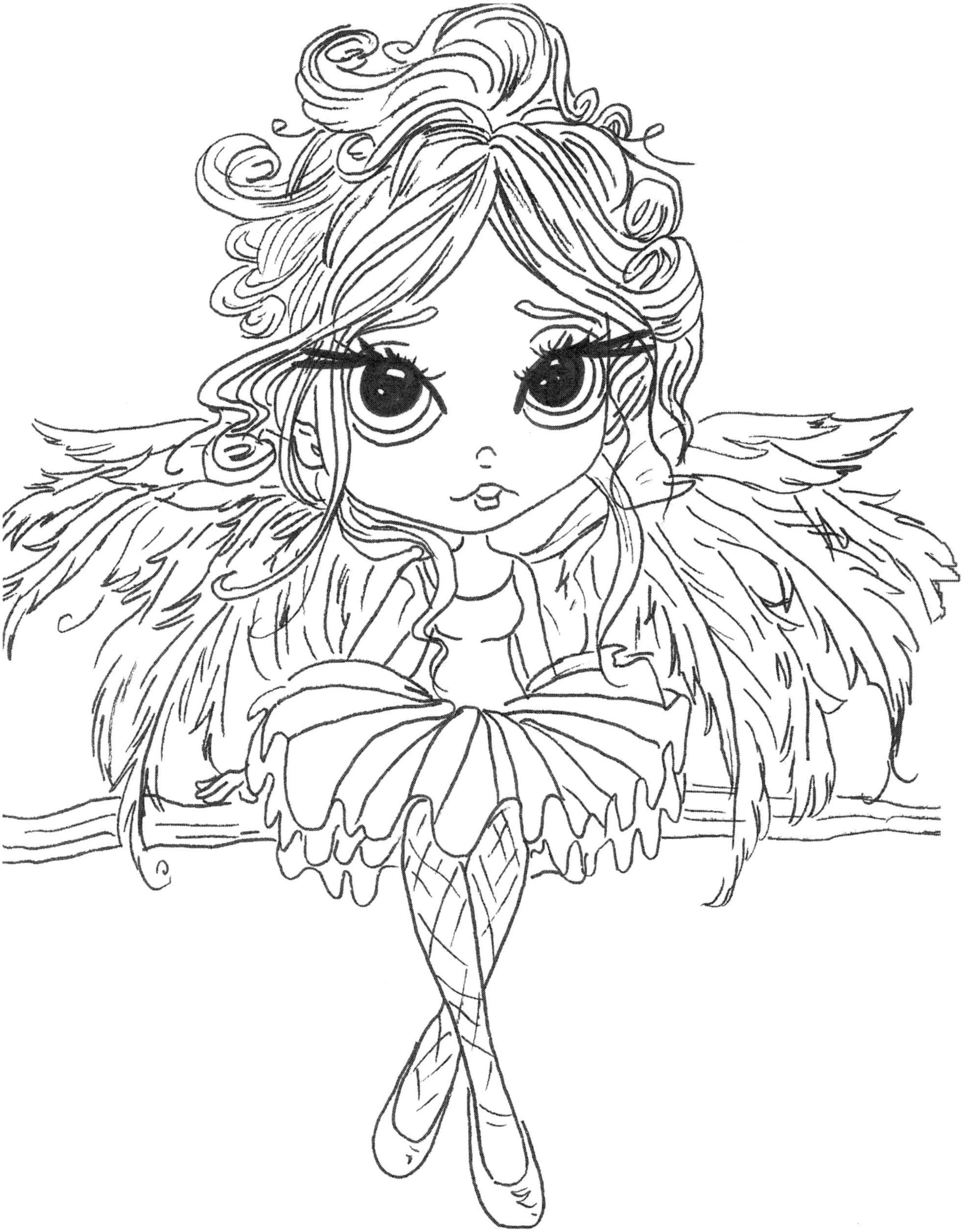

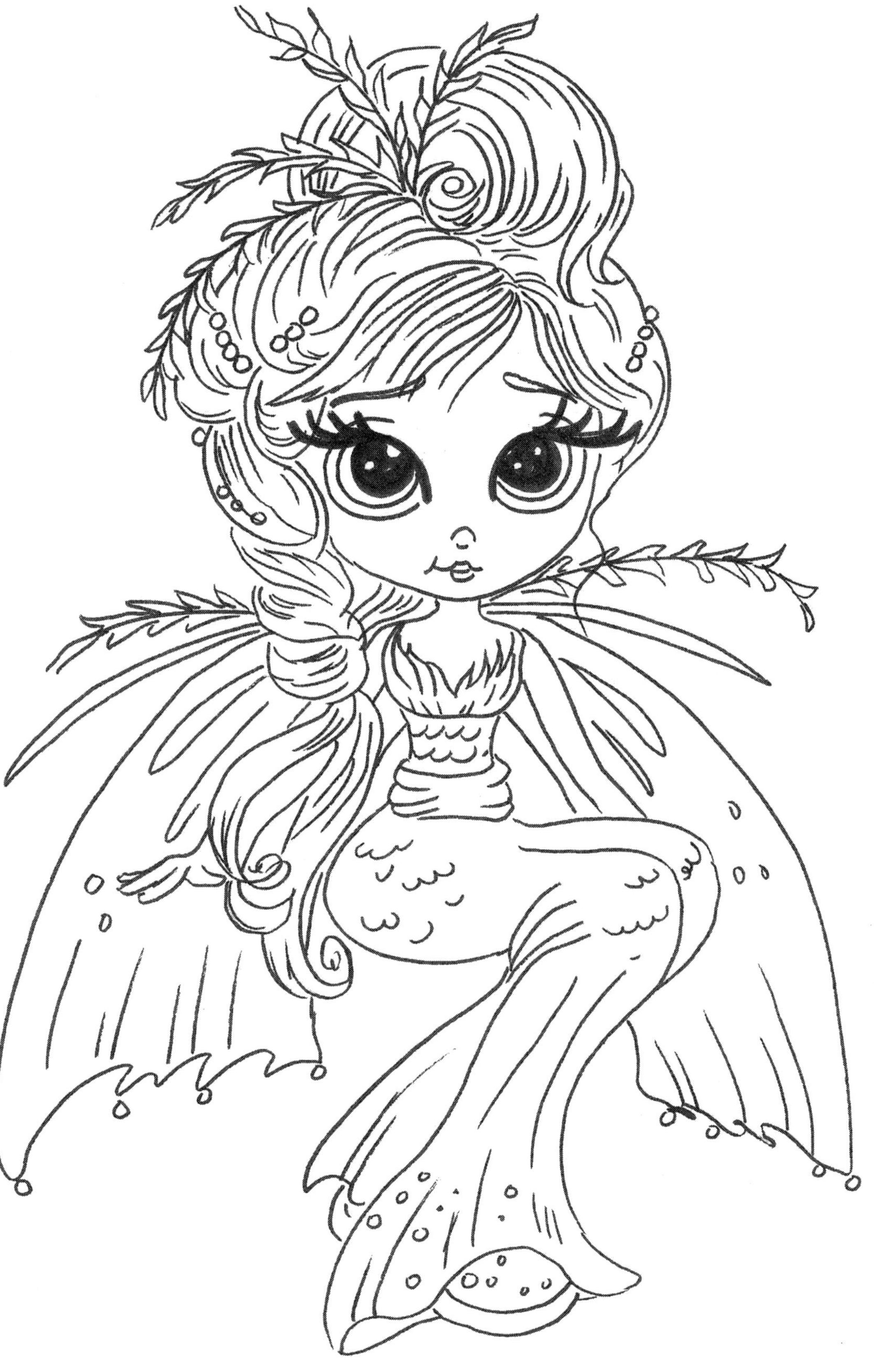

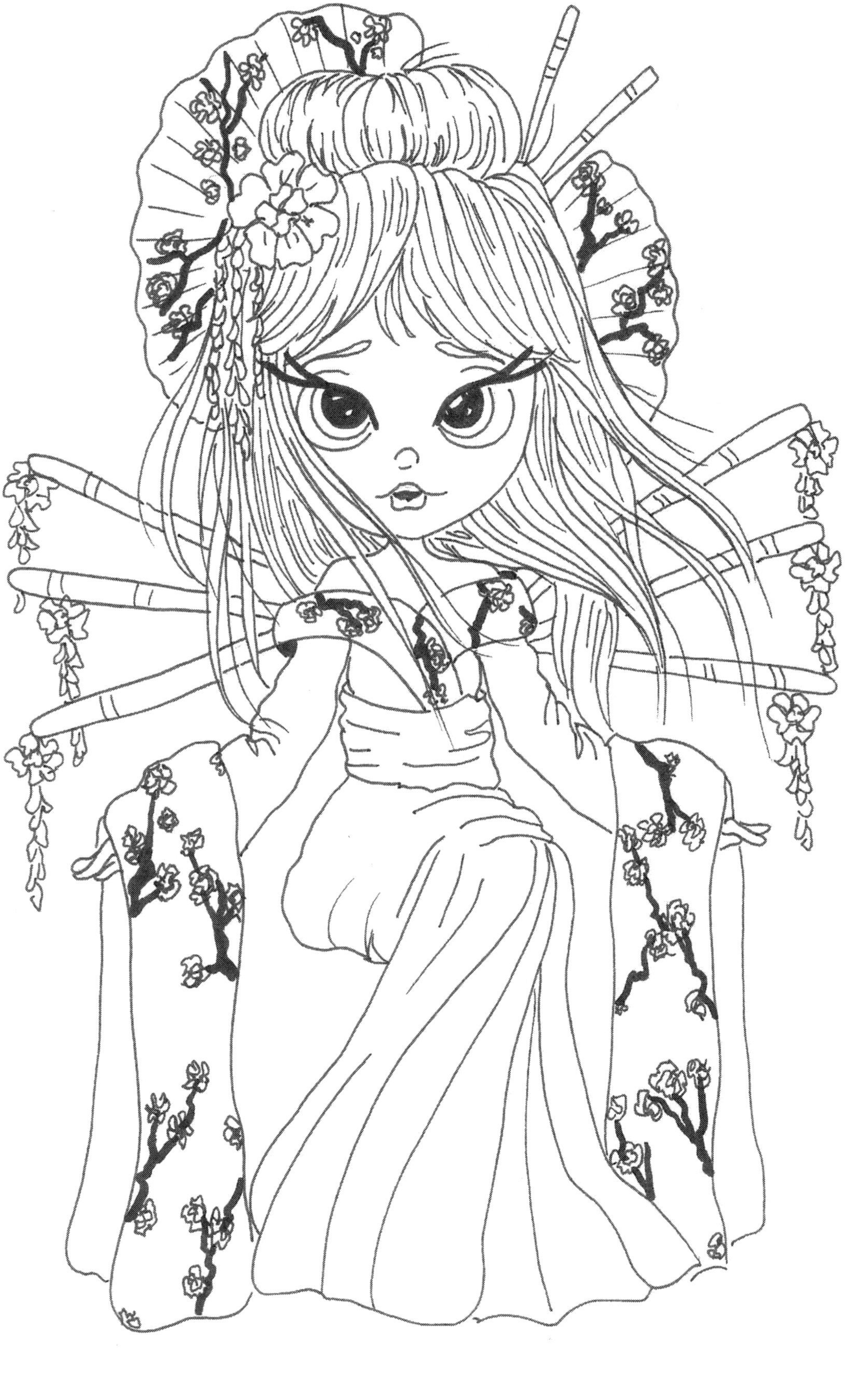

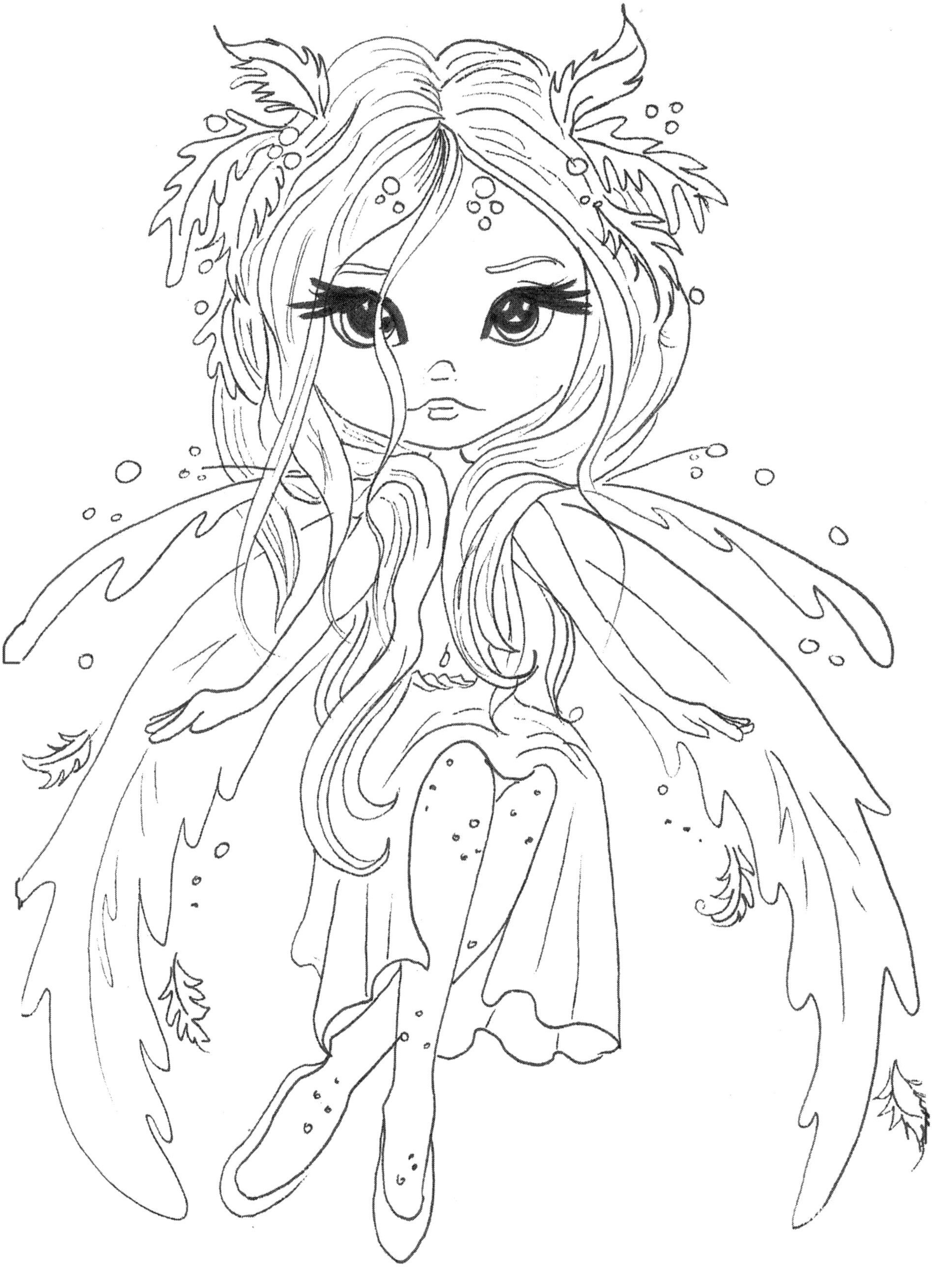

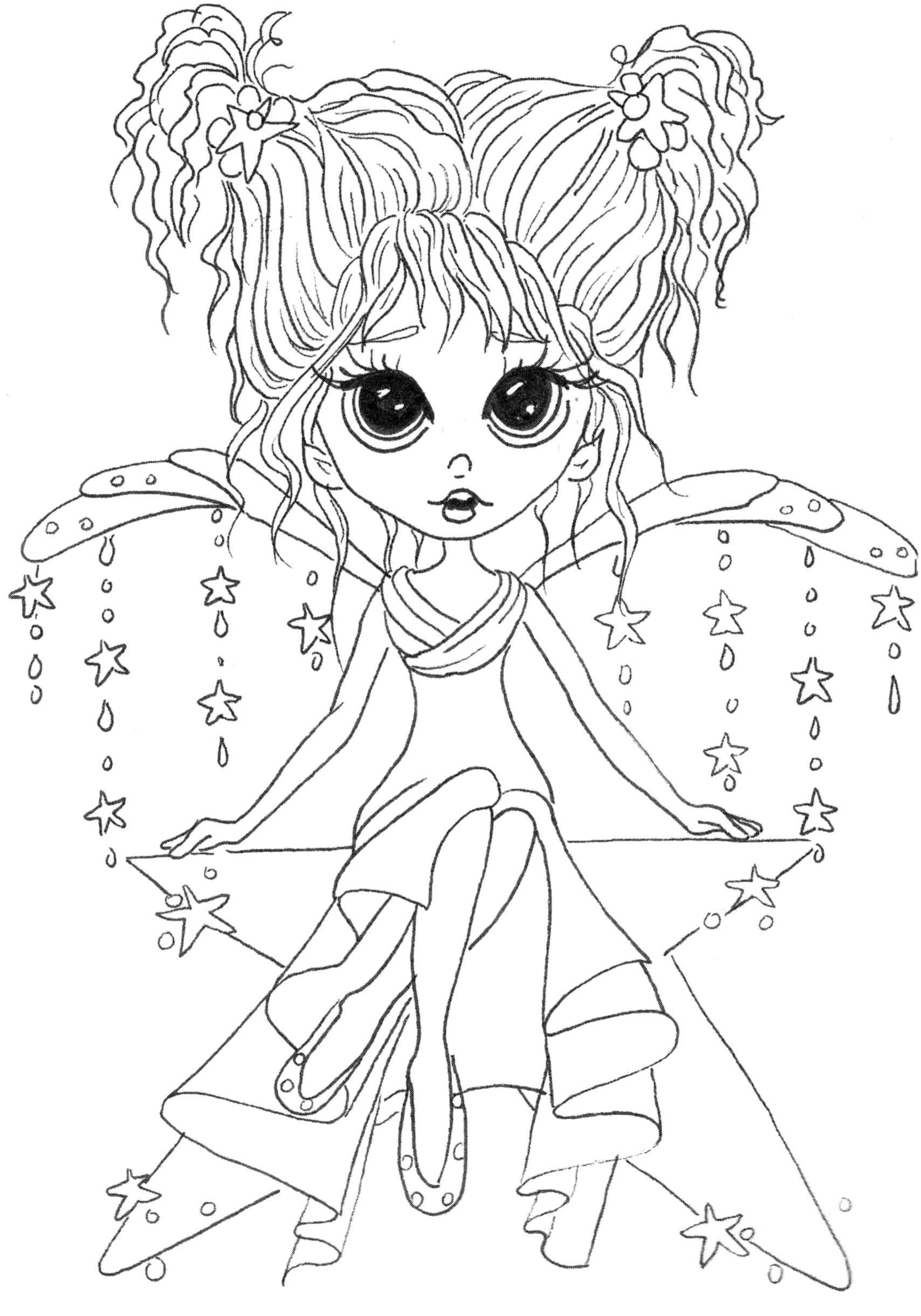

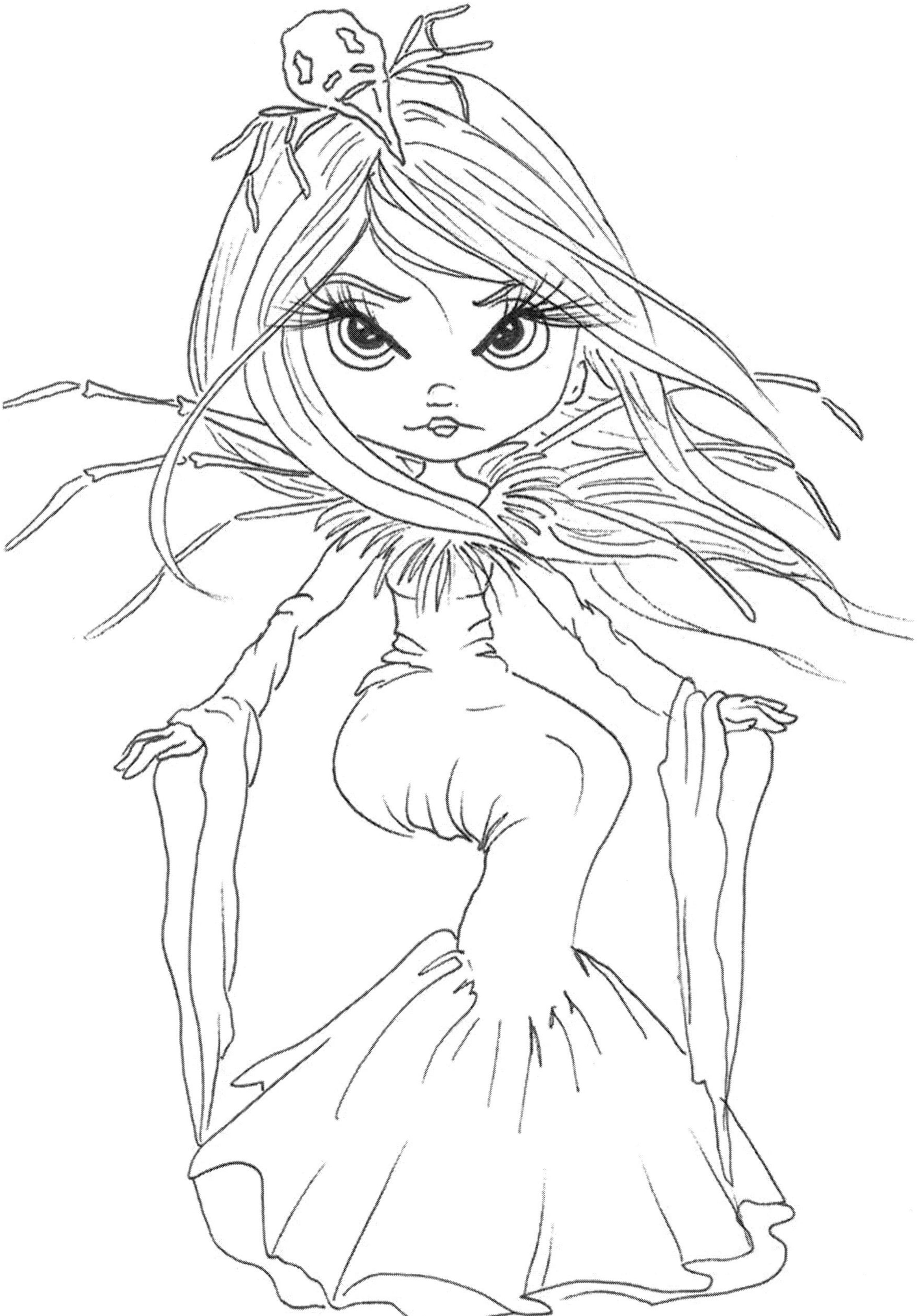

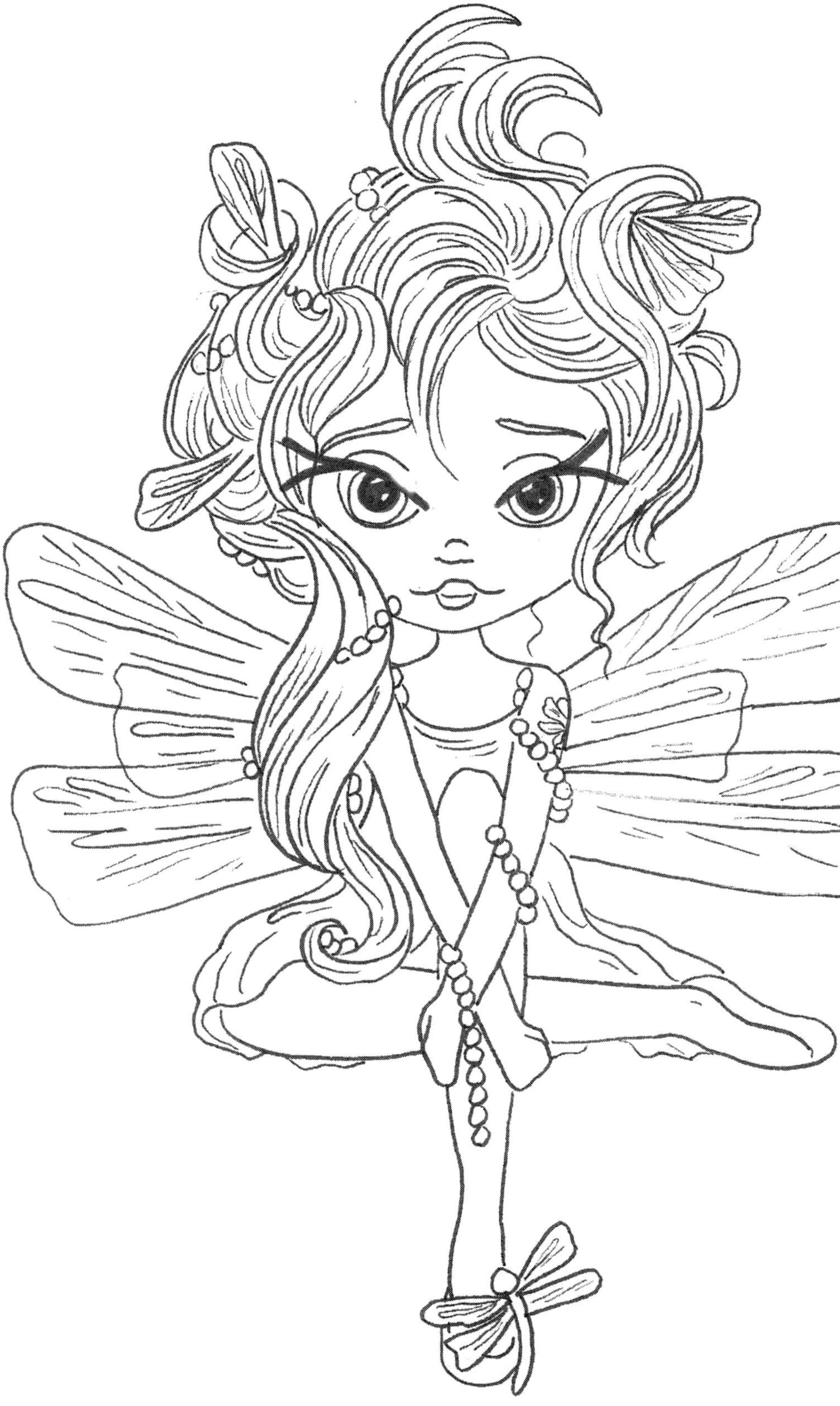

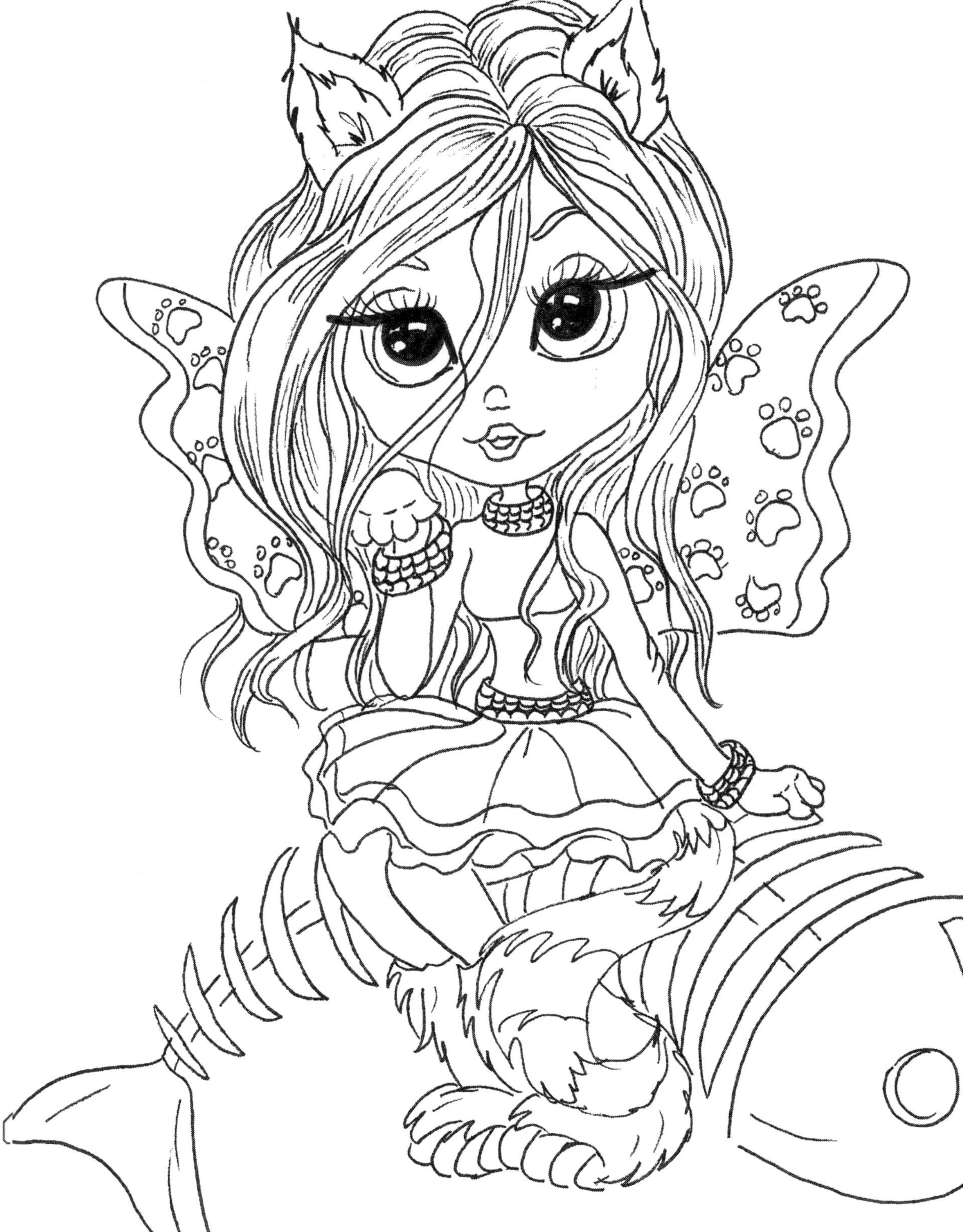

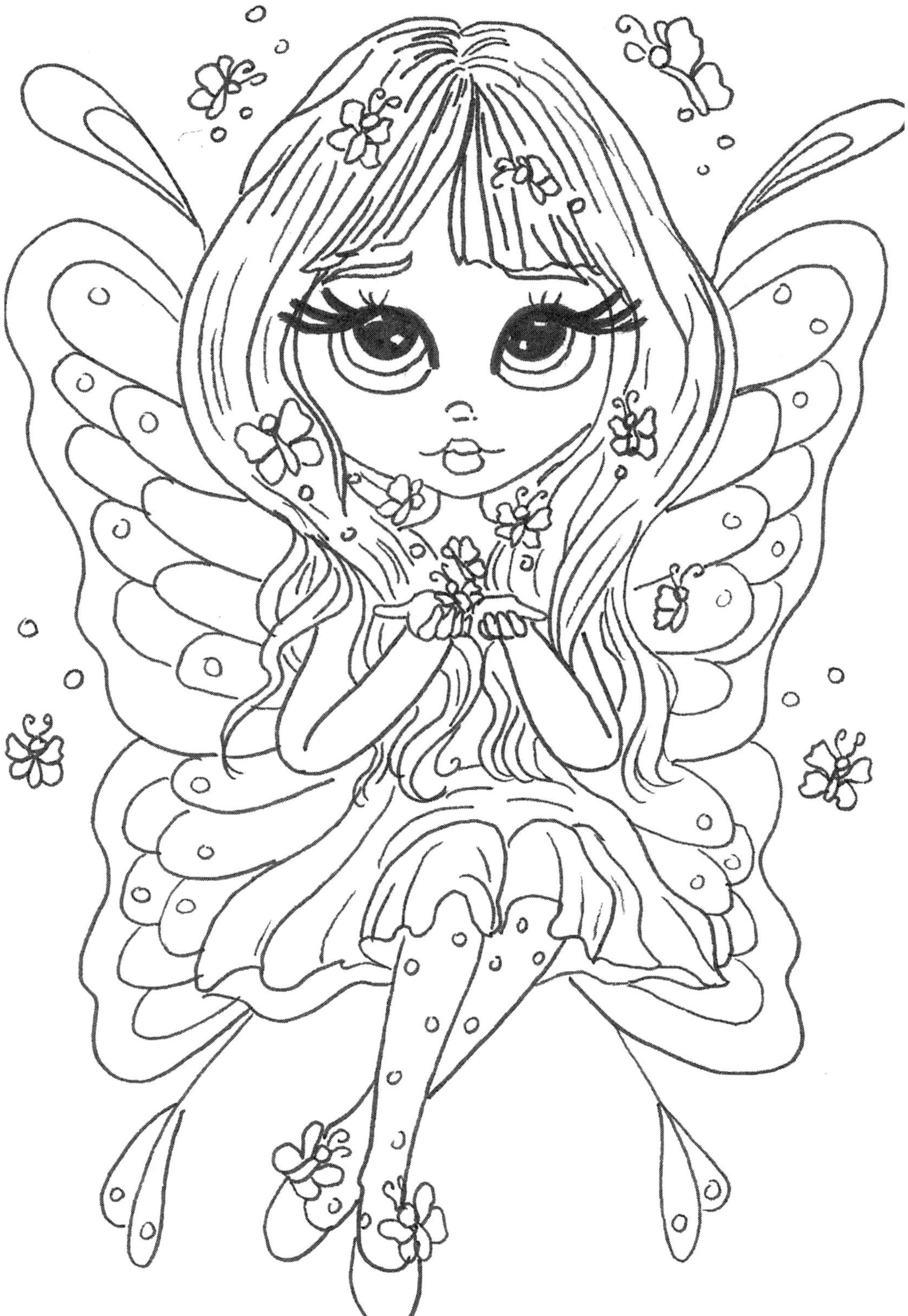

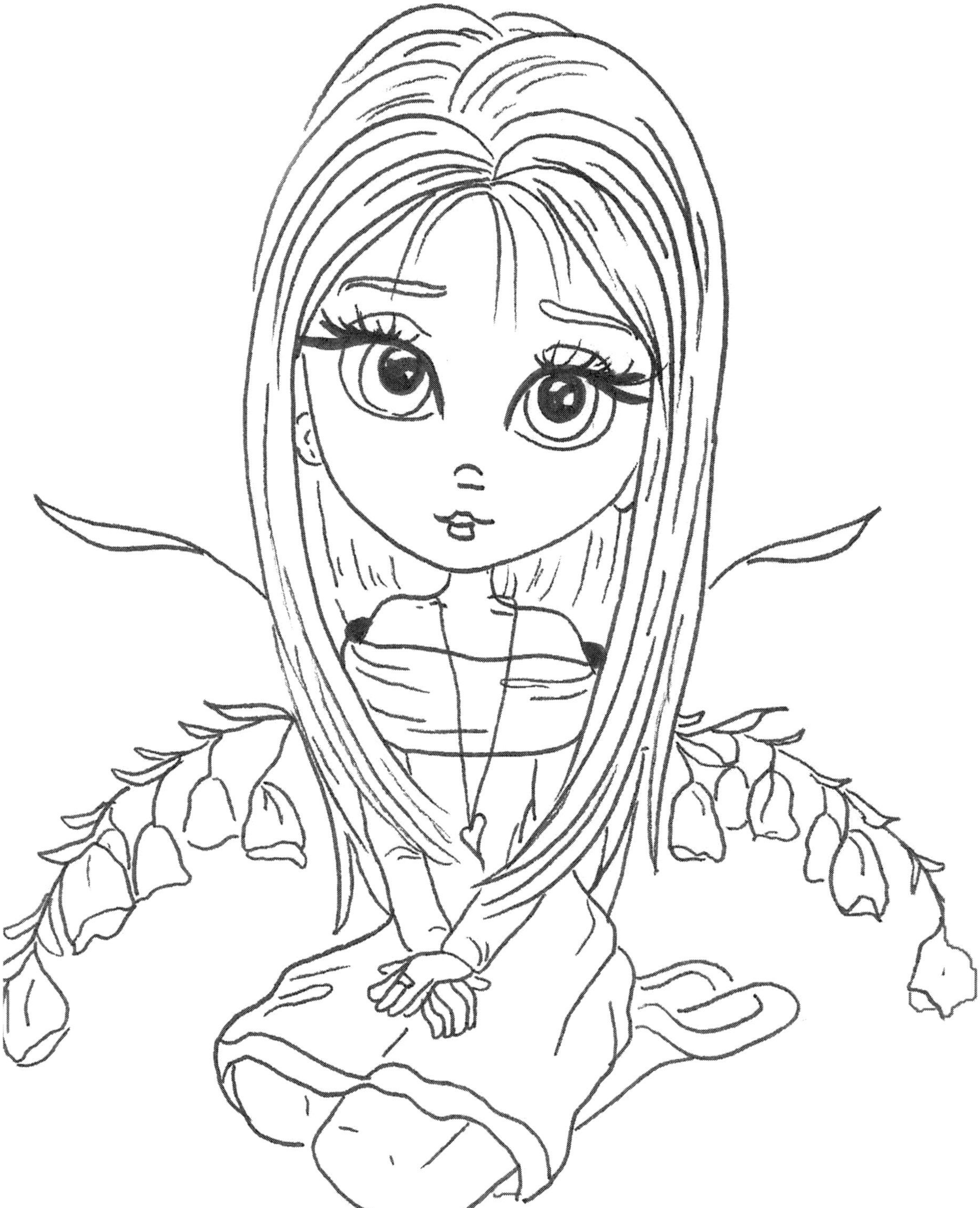

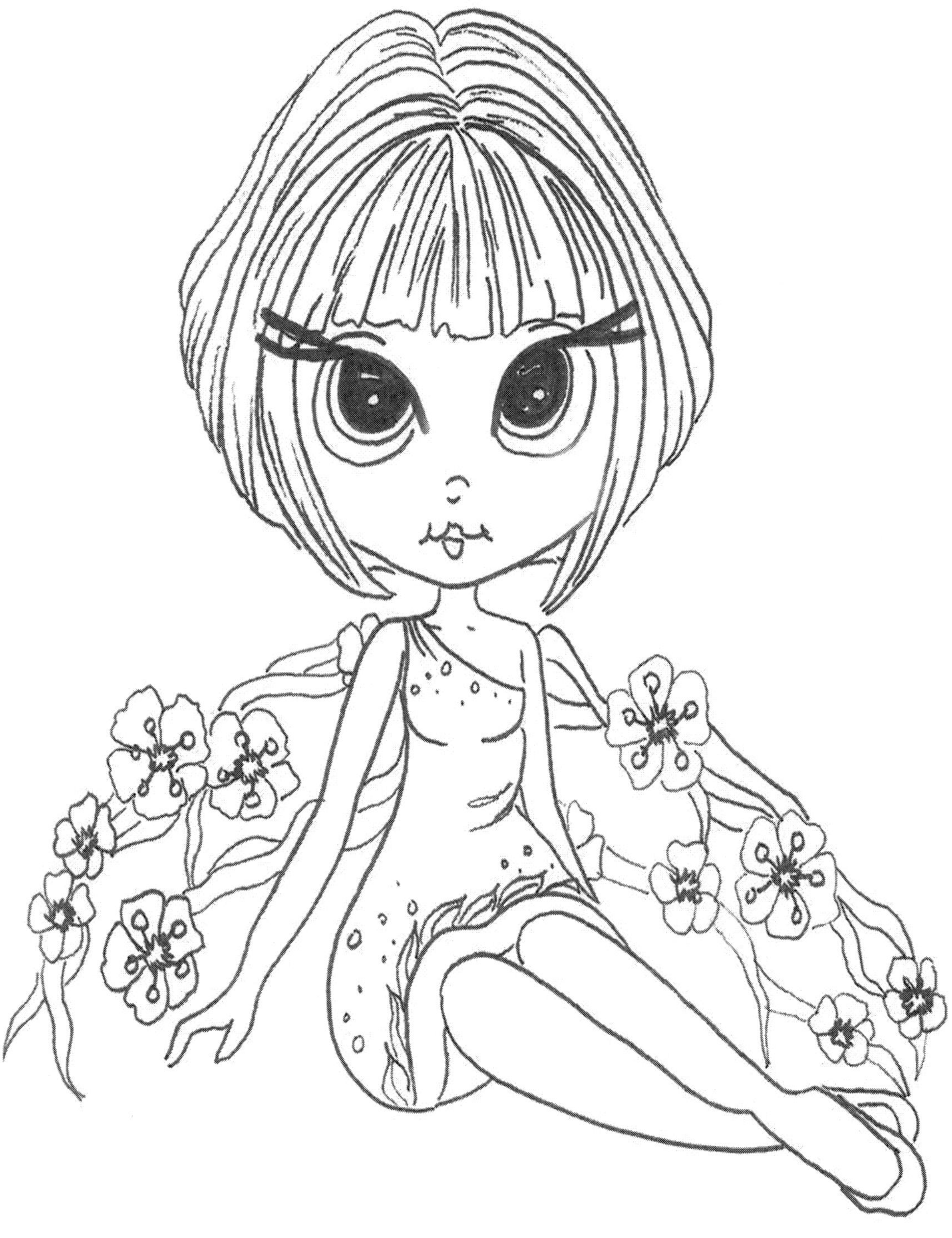

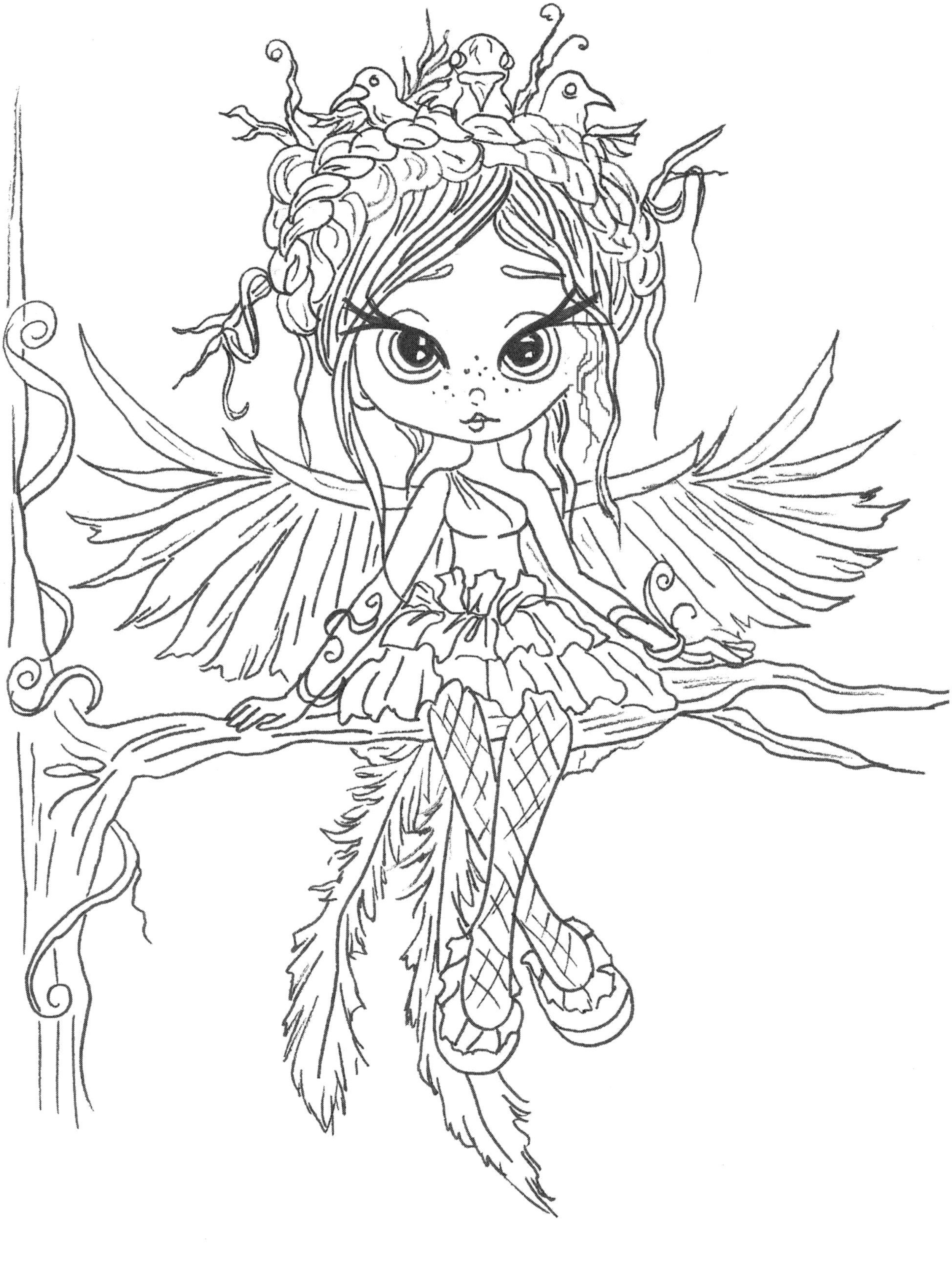

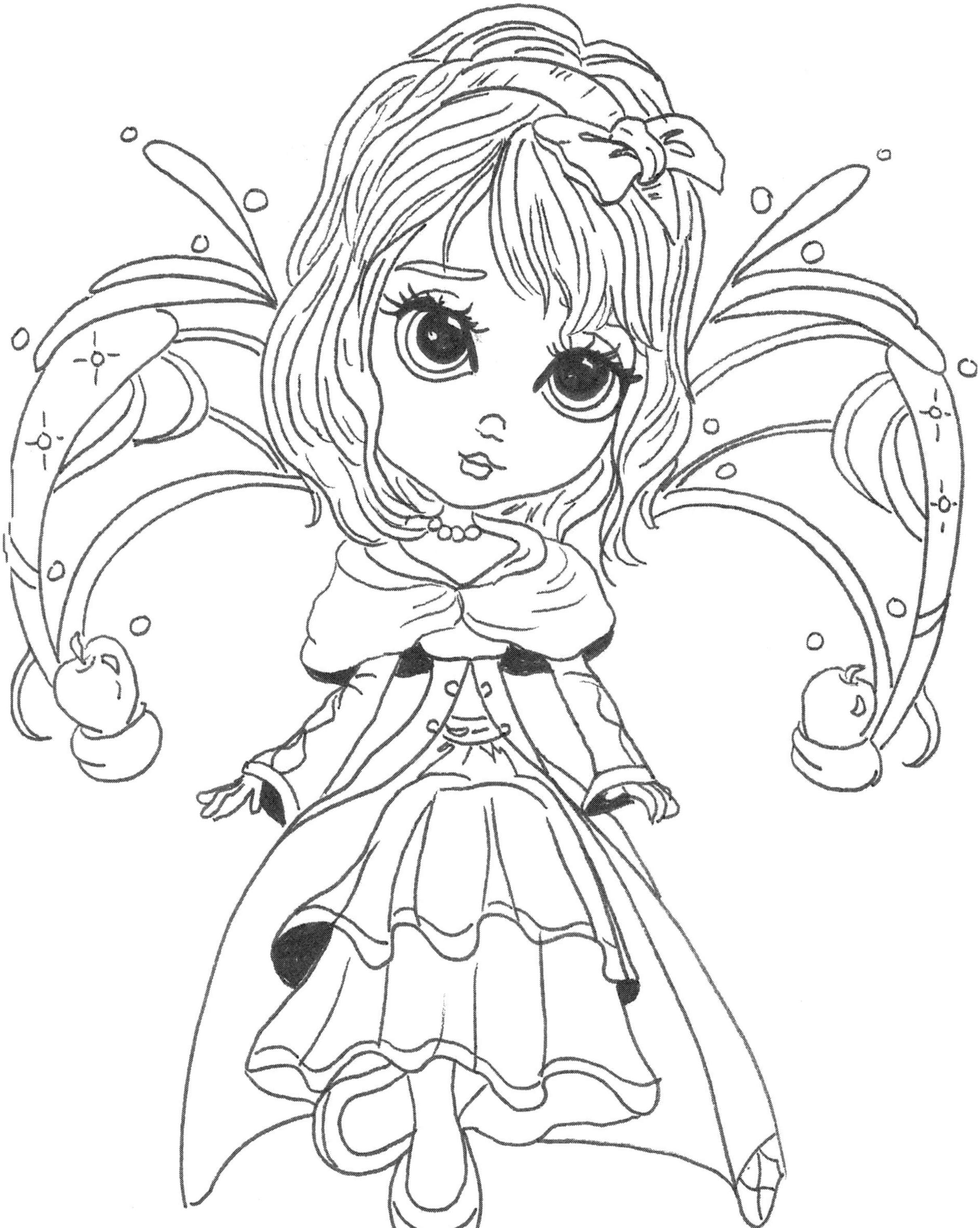

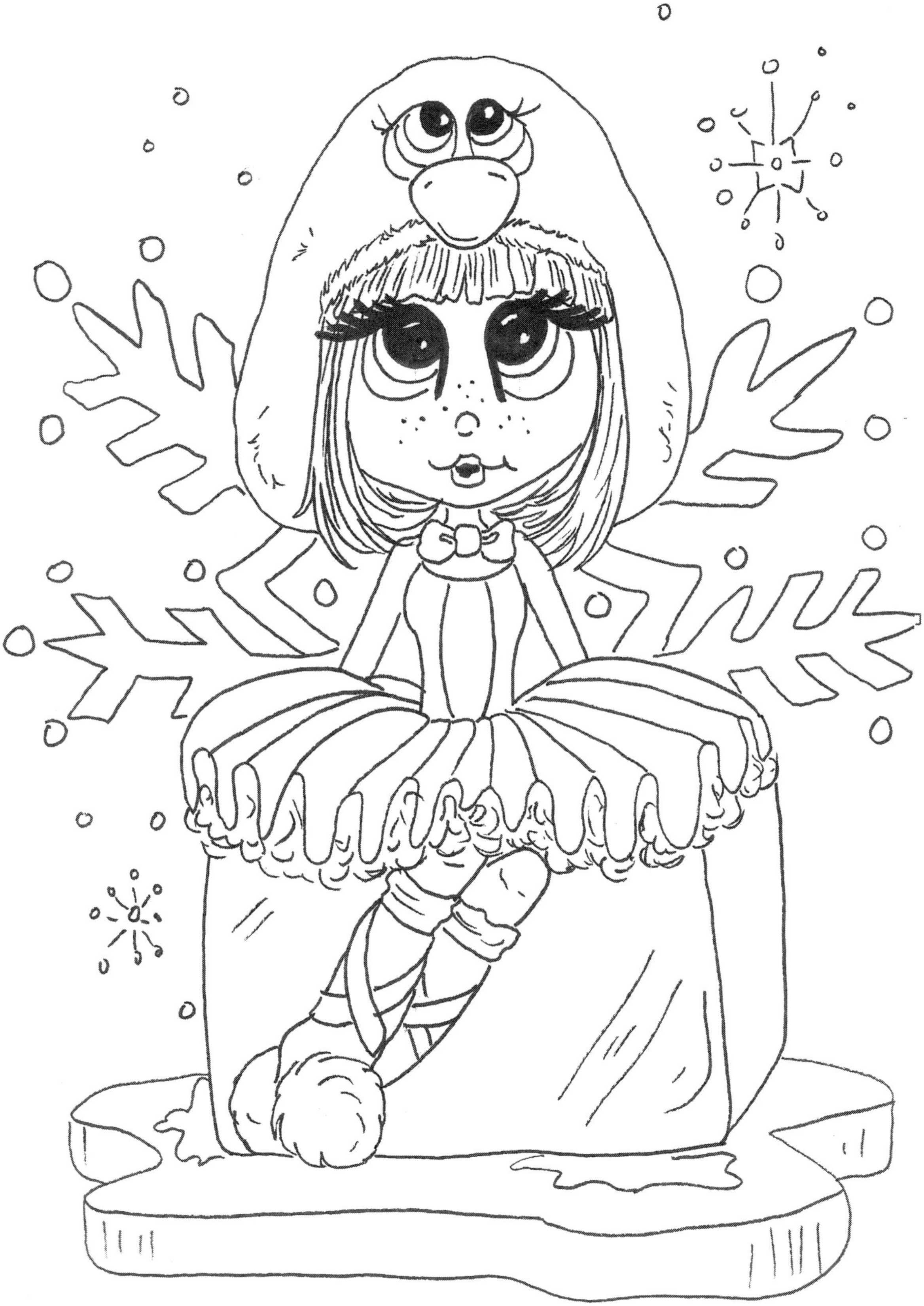

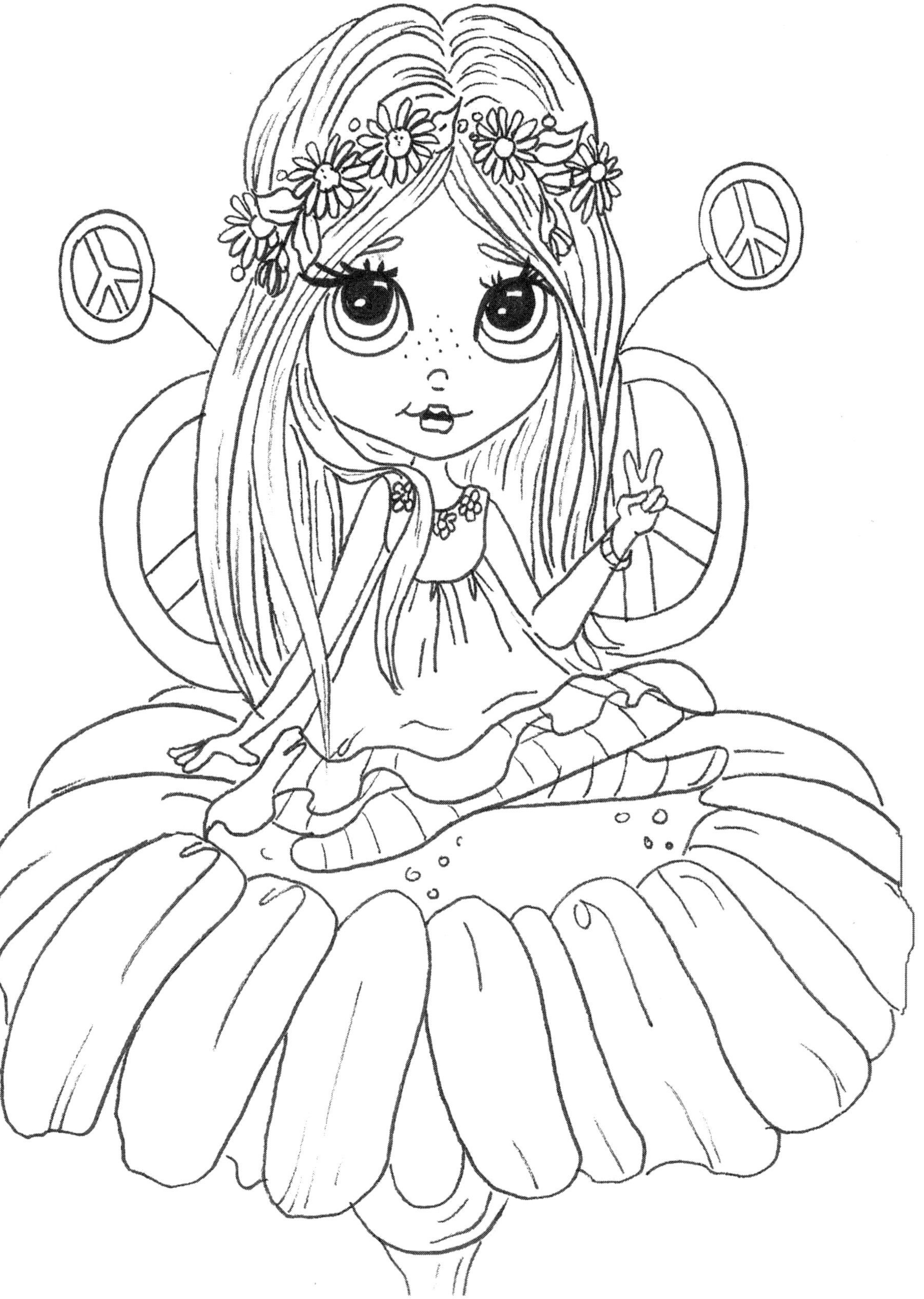

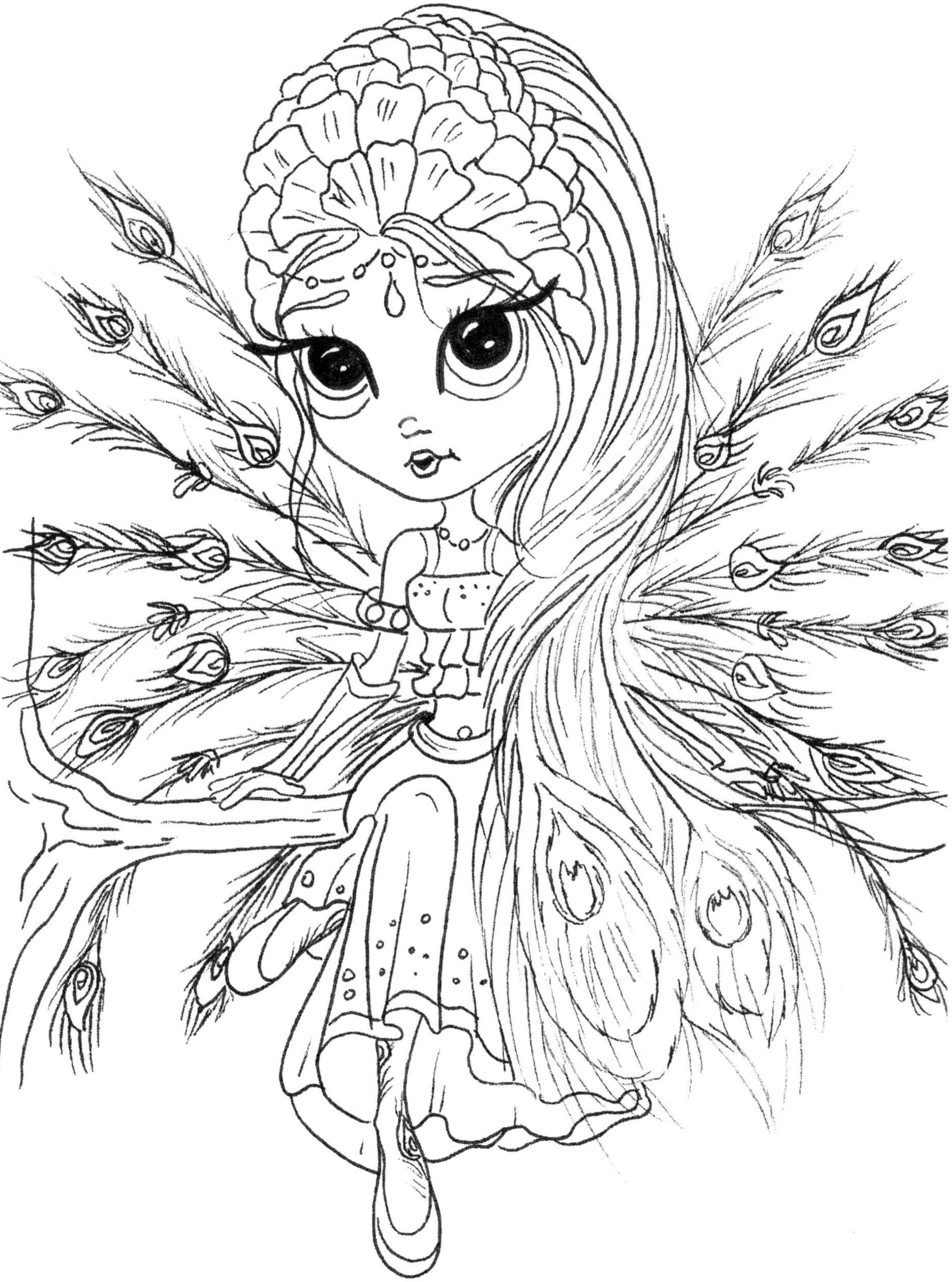

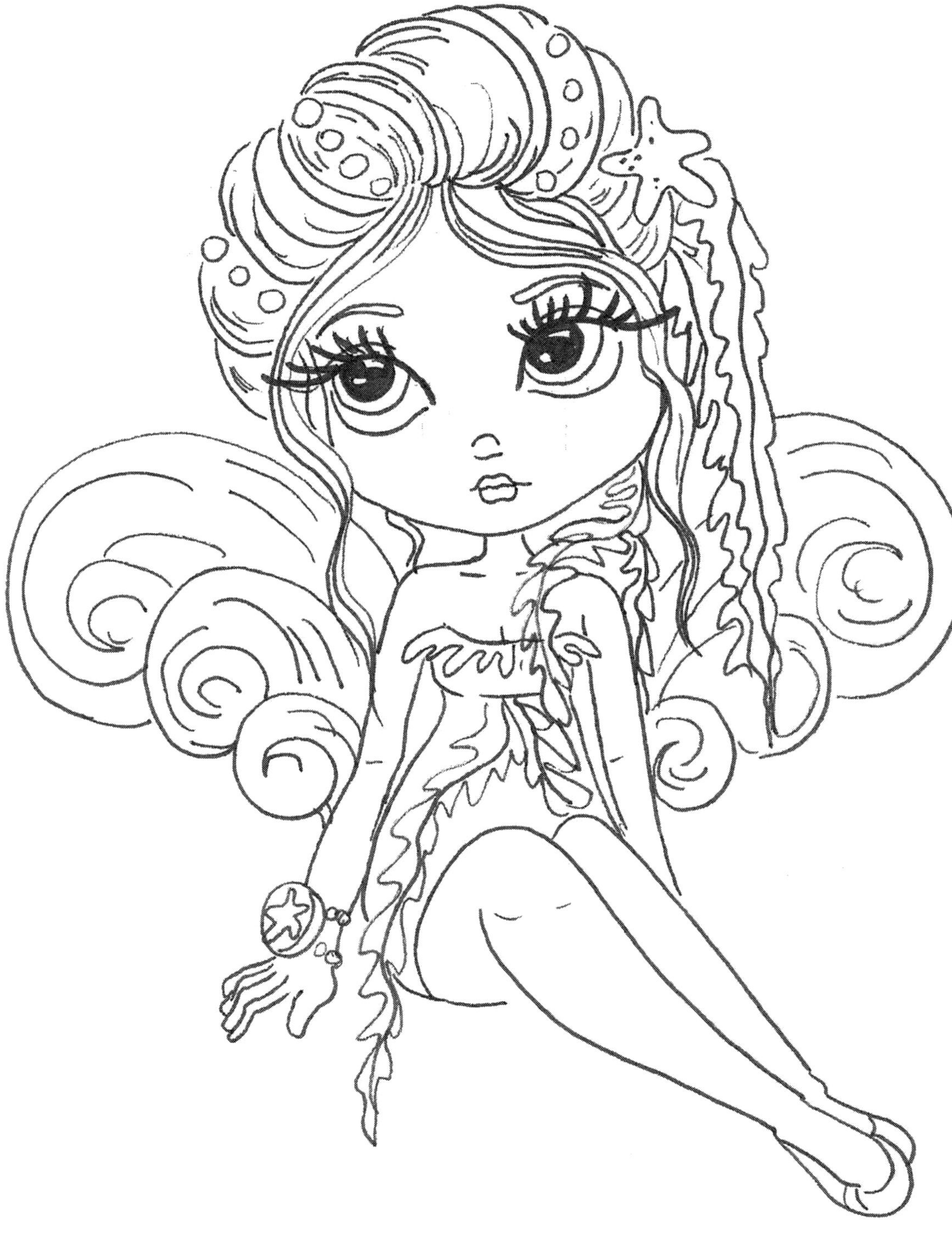

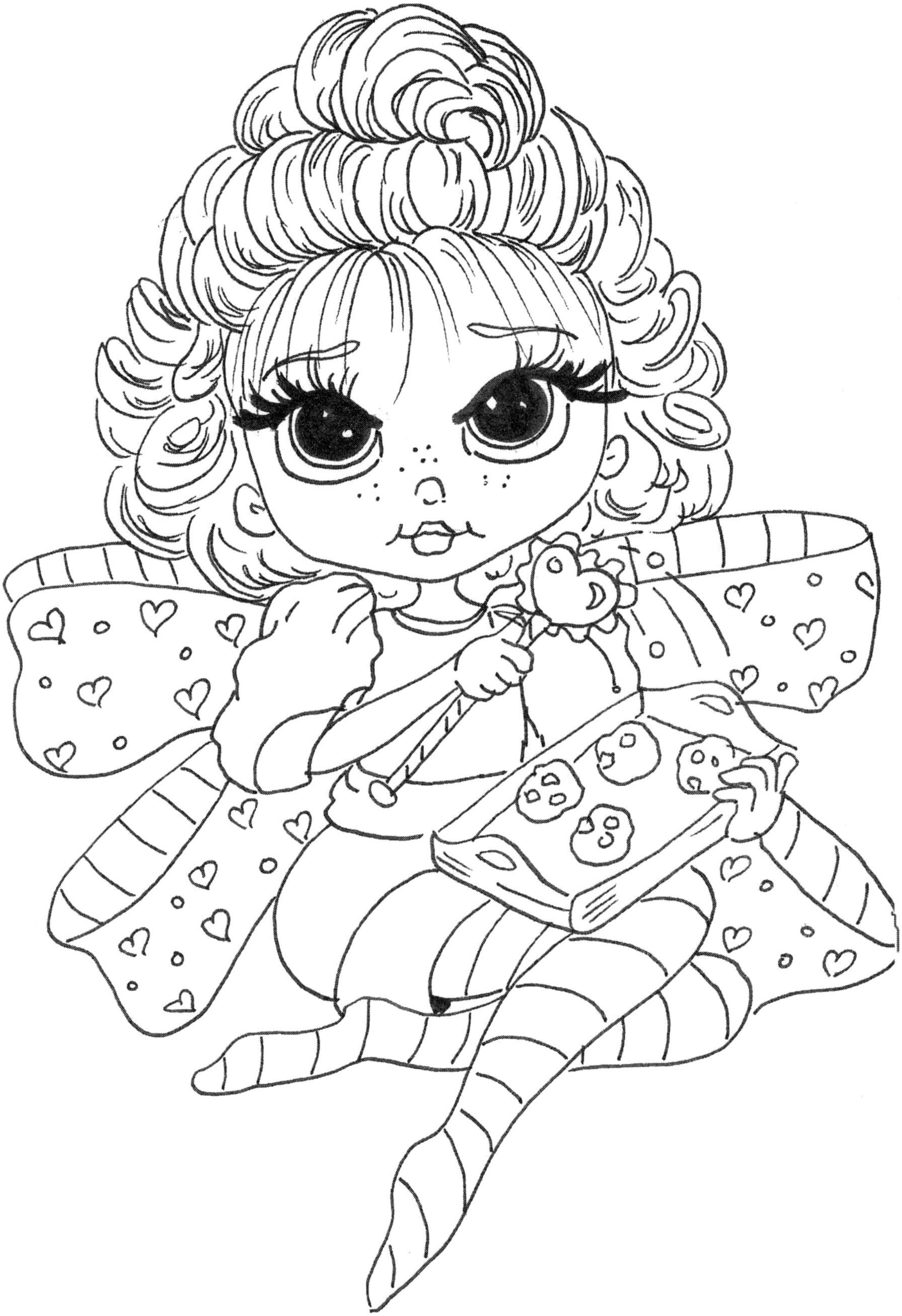

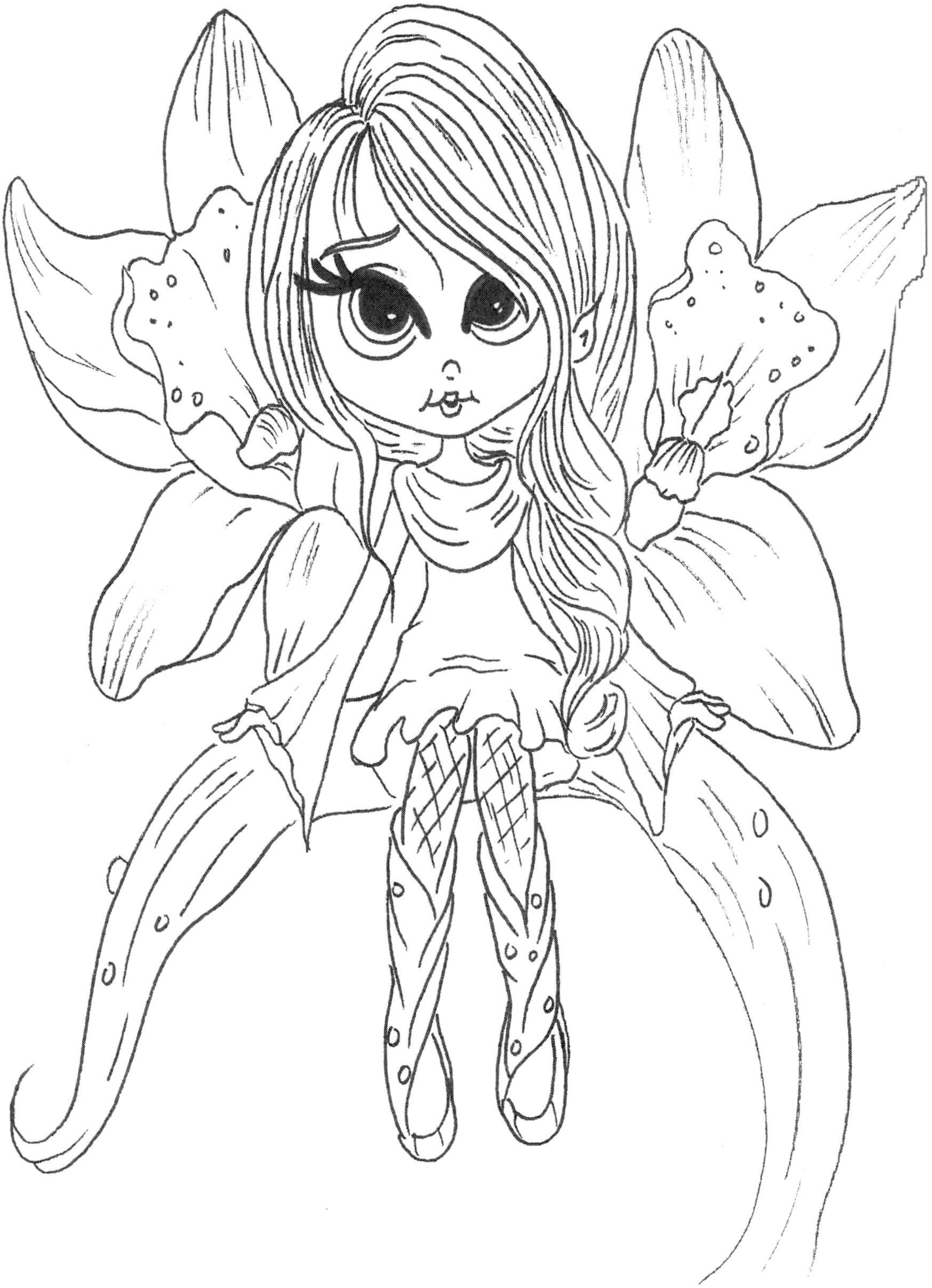

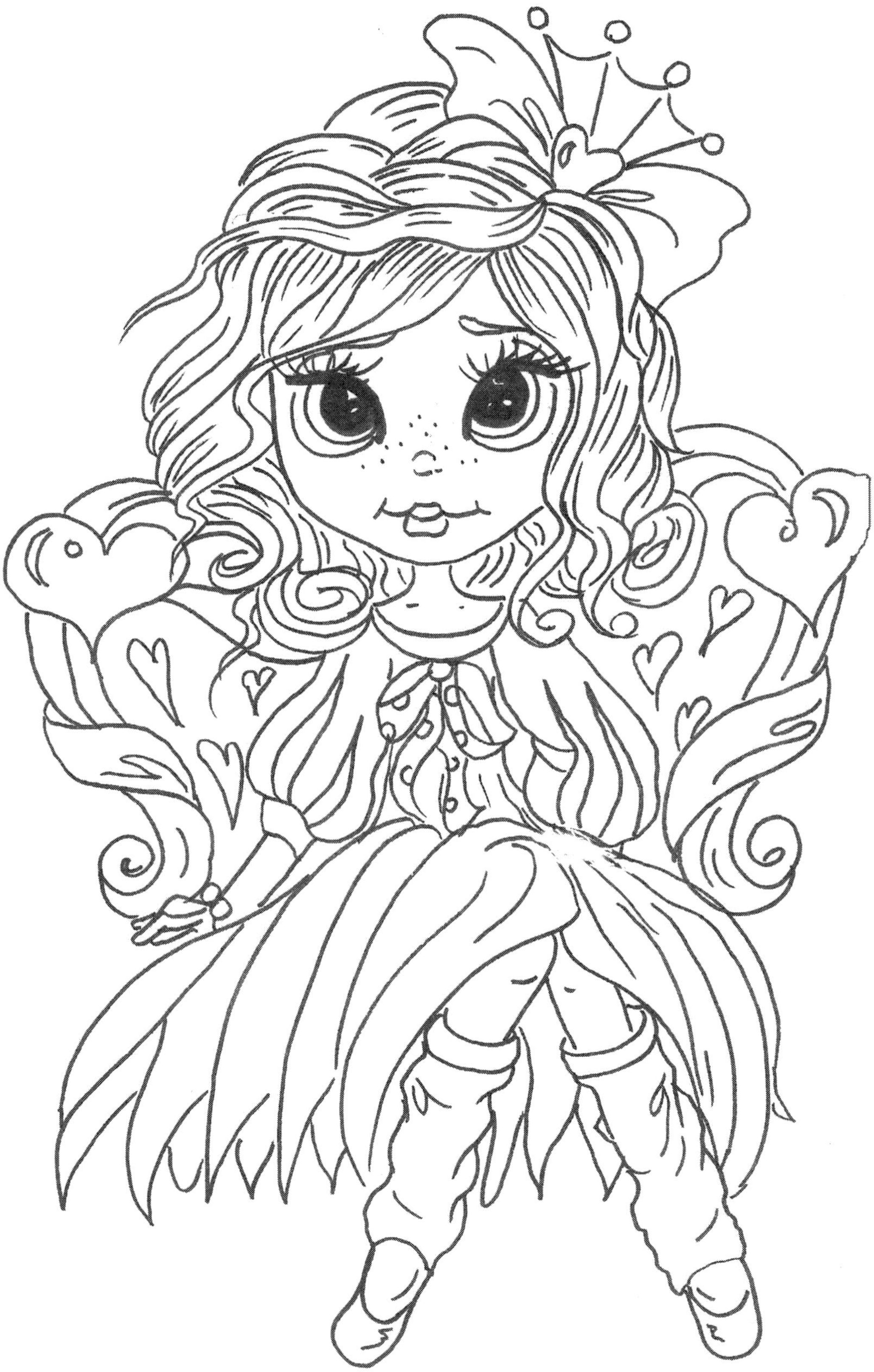

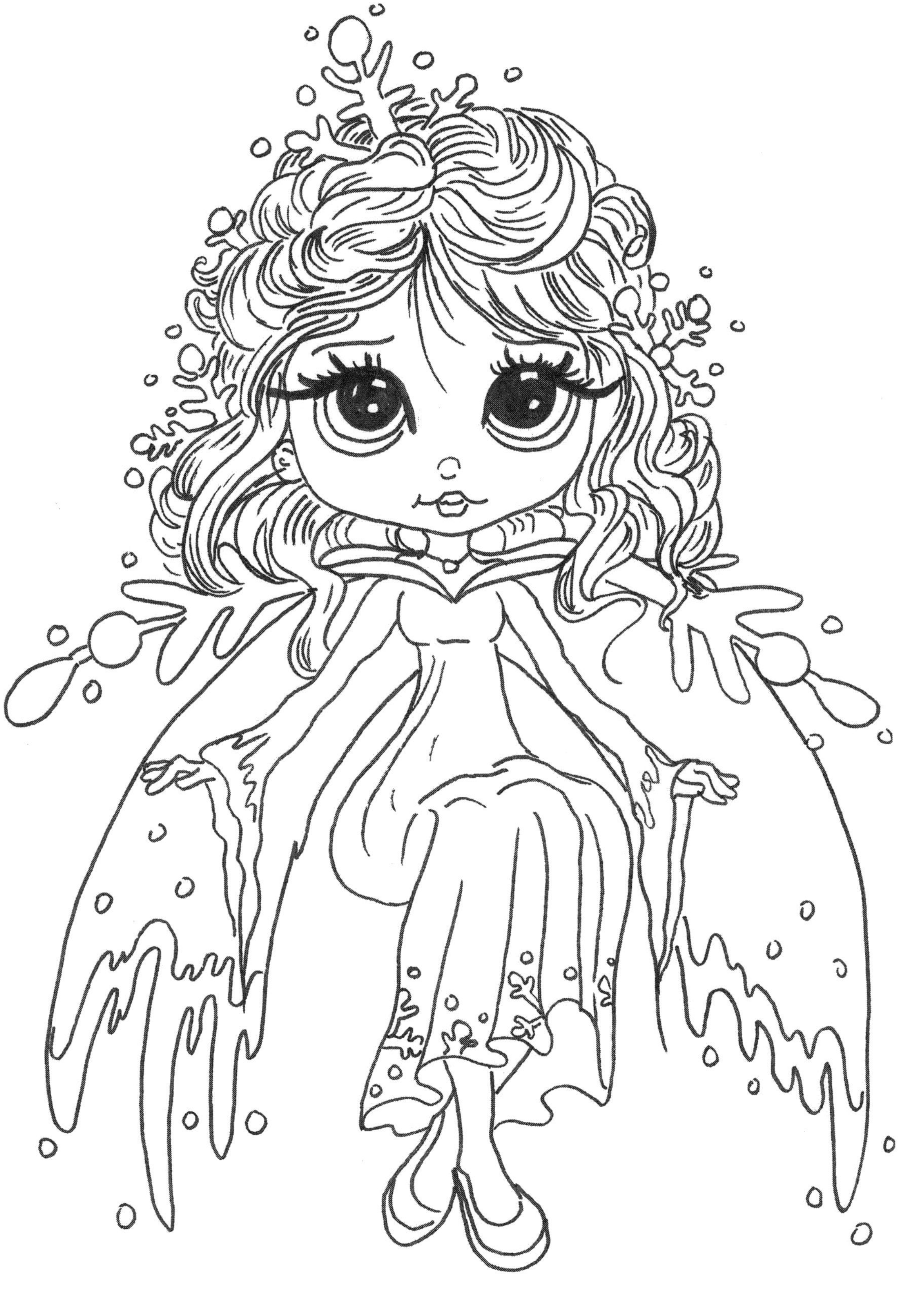

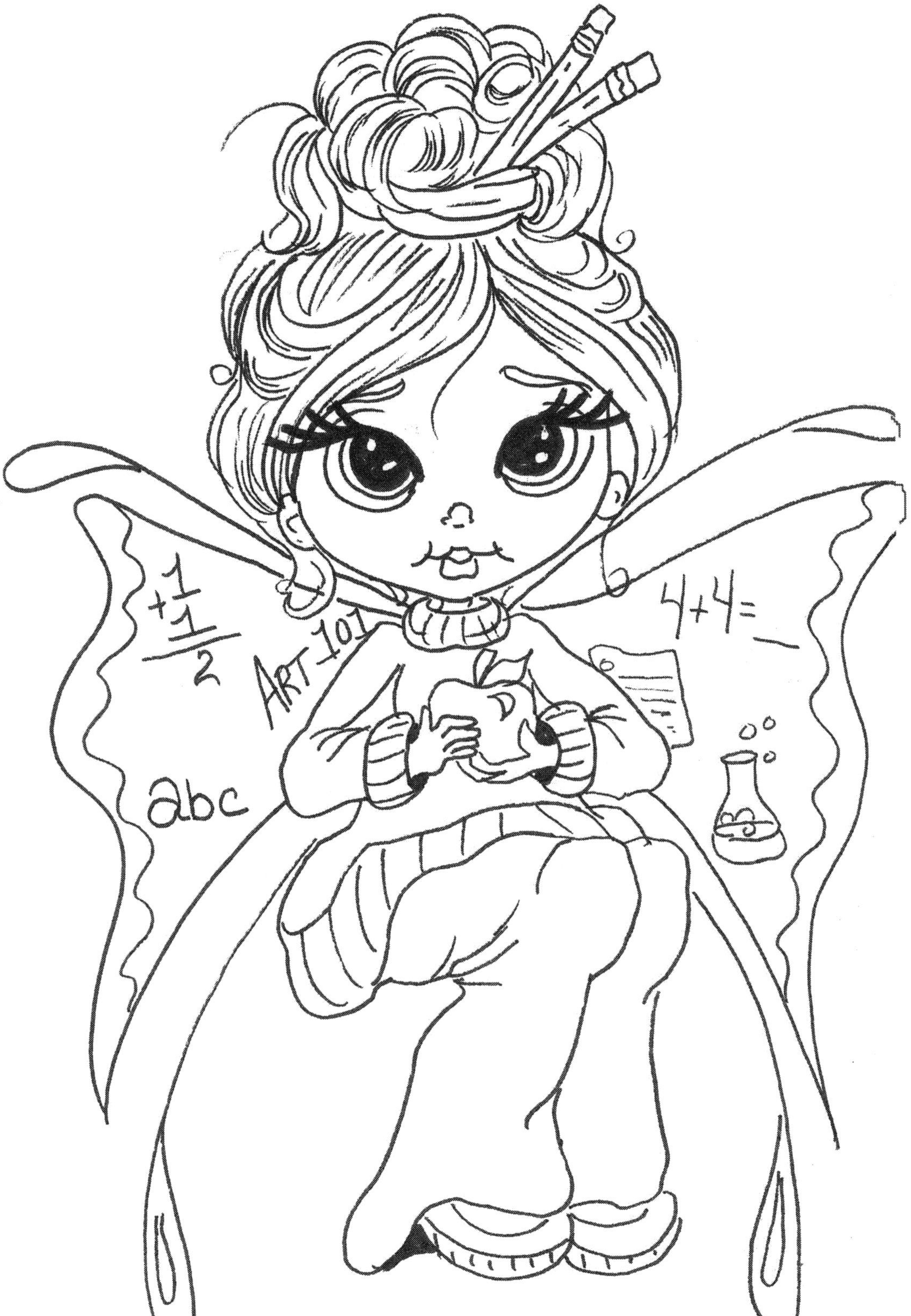

+1
1
2
ART 101
abc
4+4=_

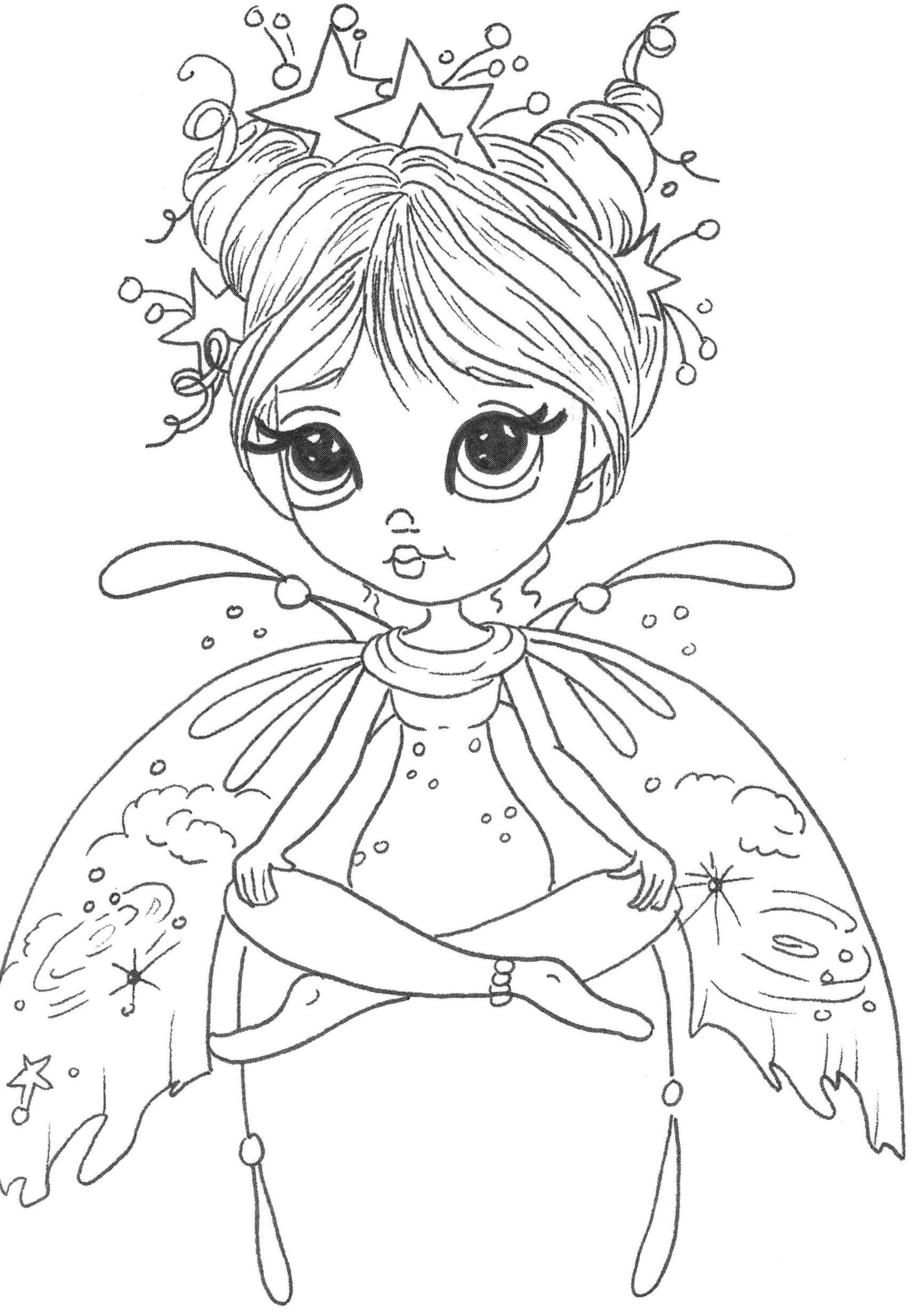

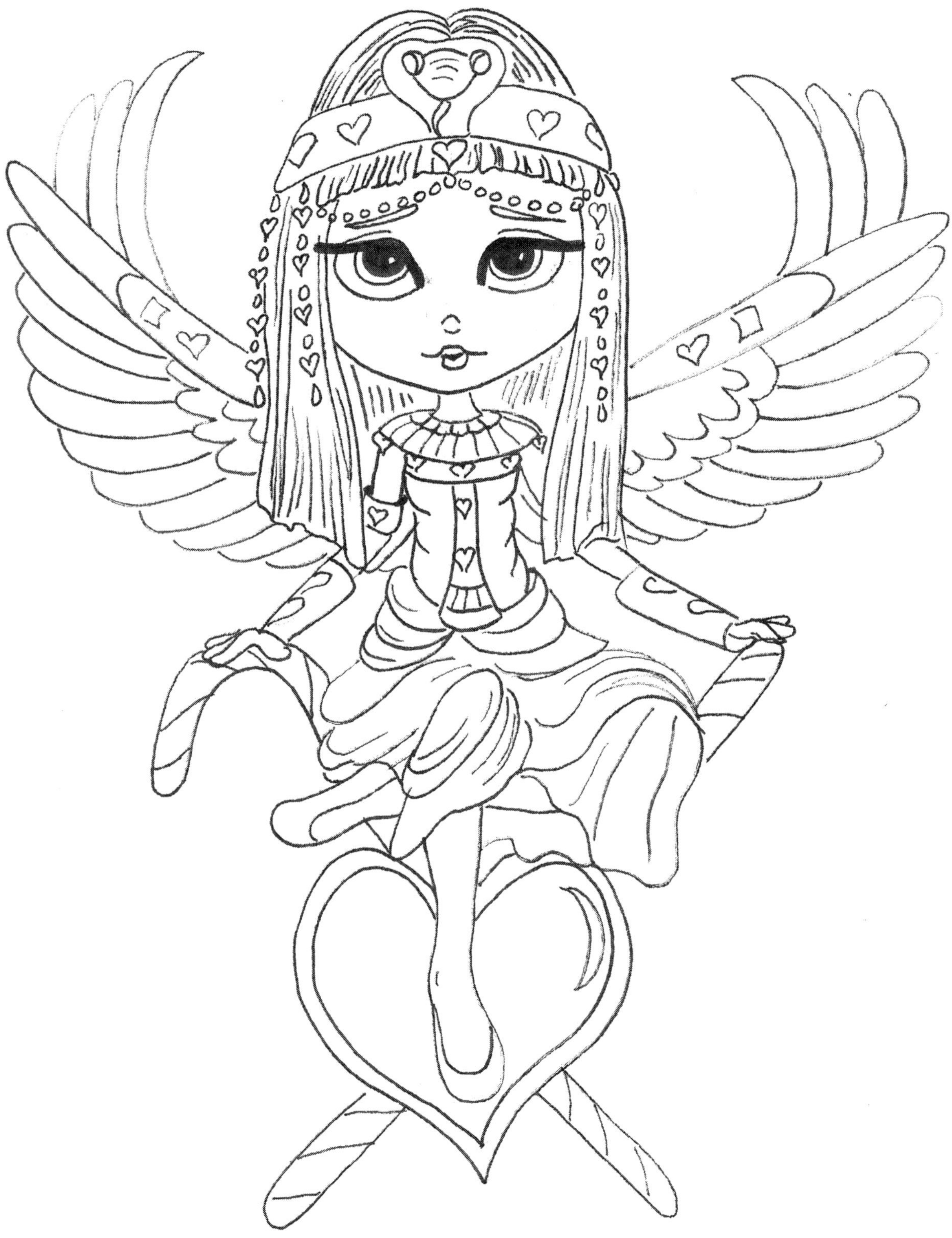

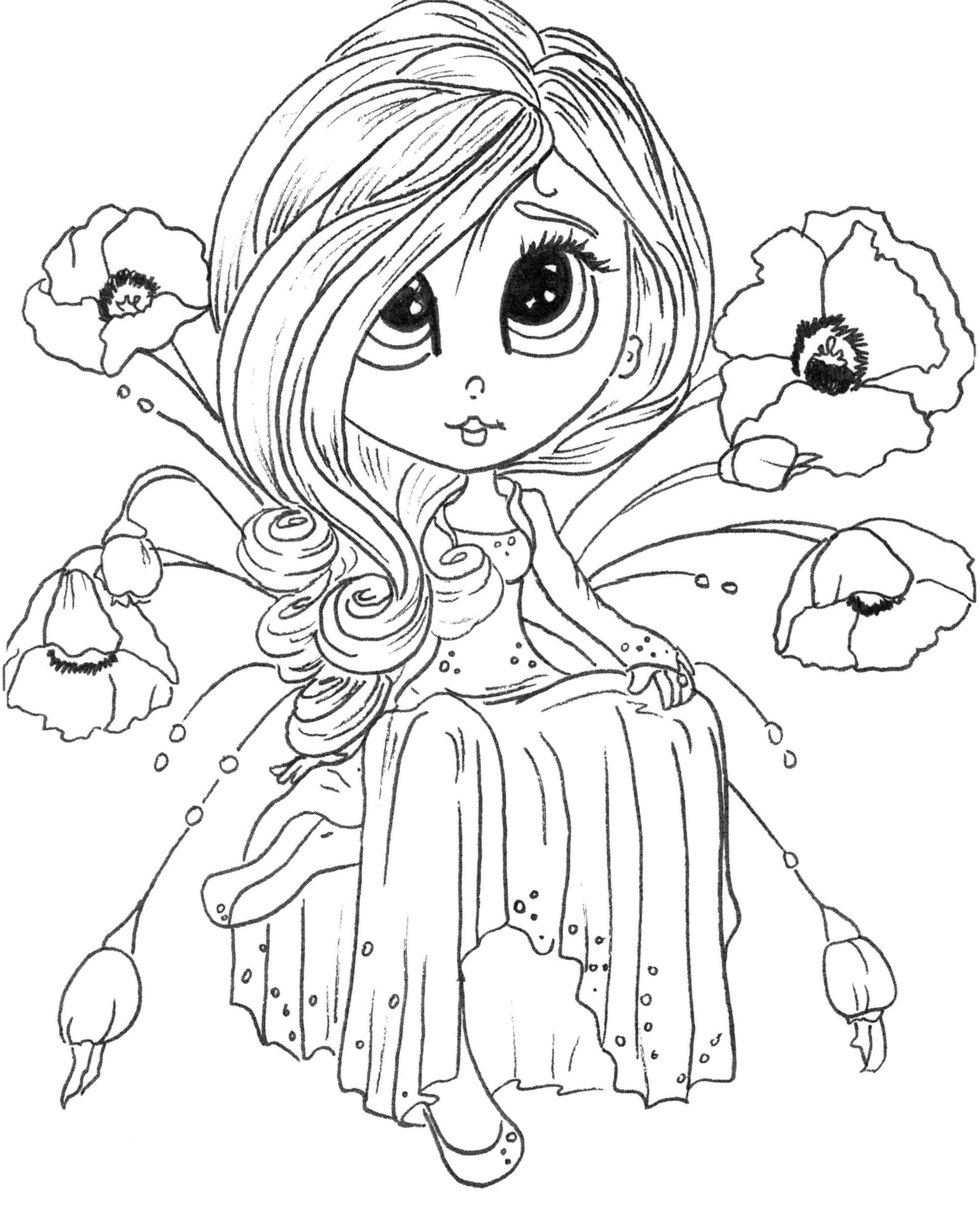

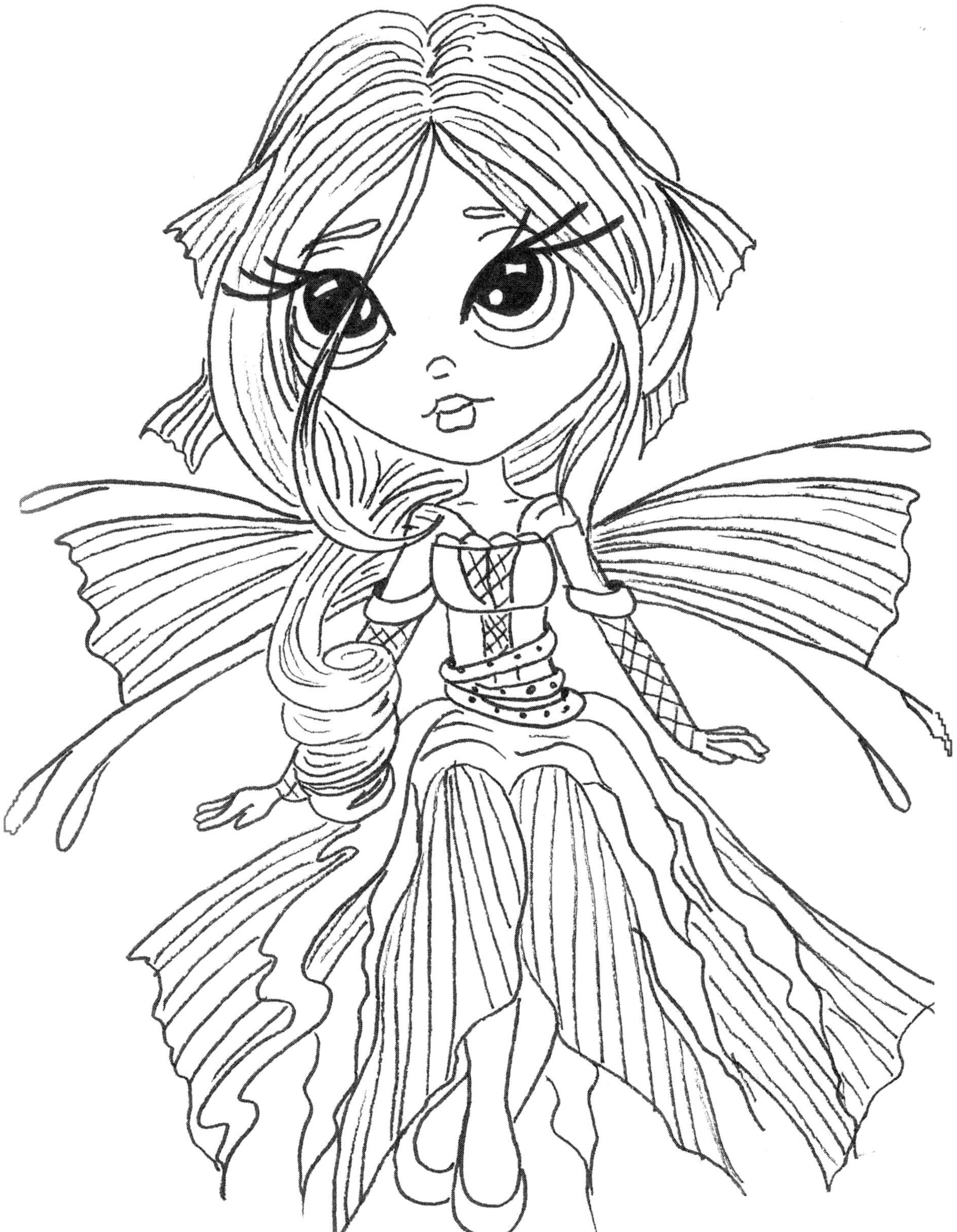

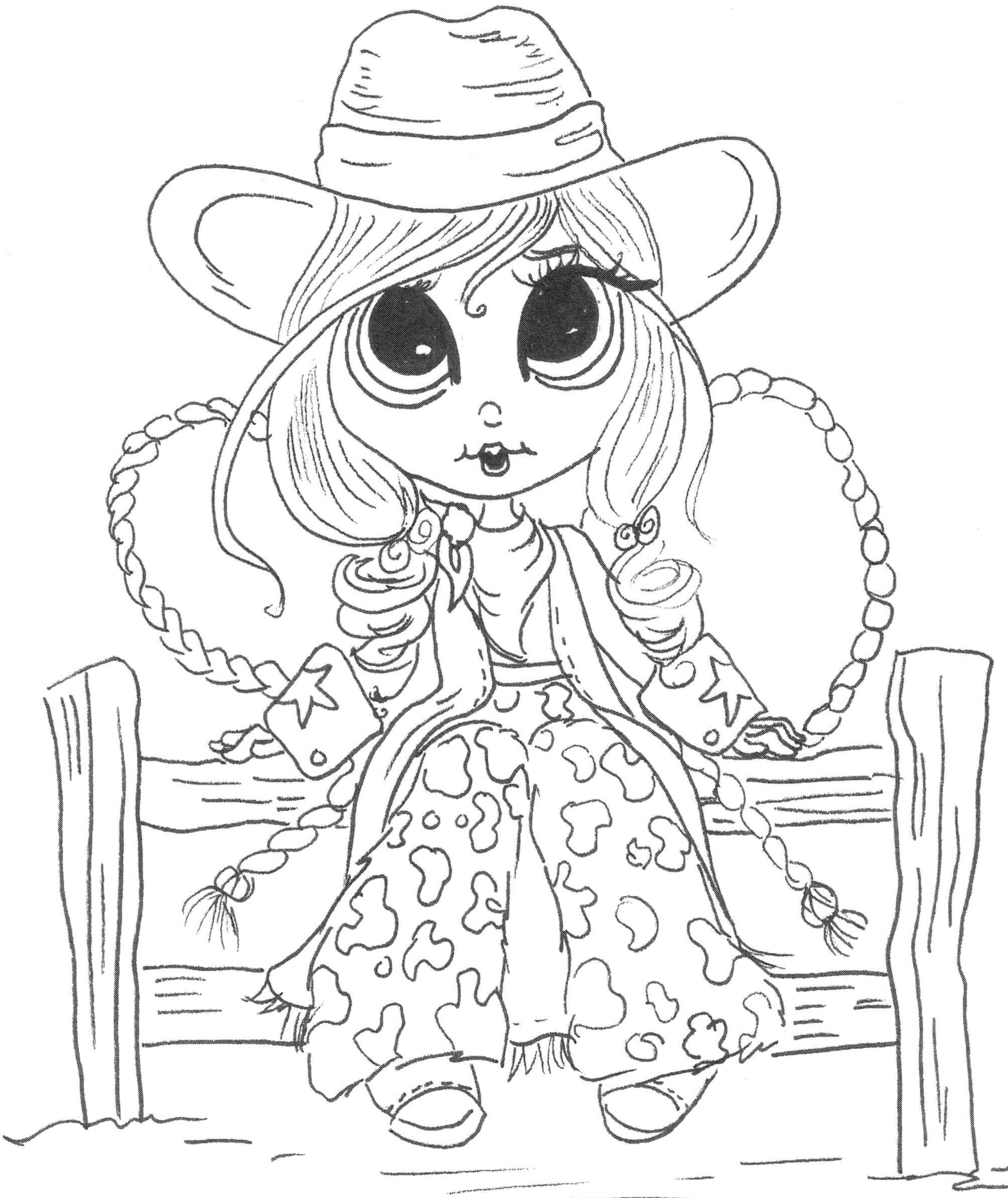

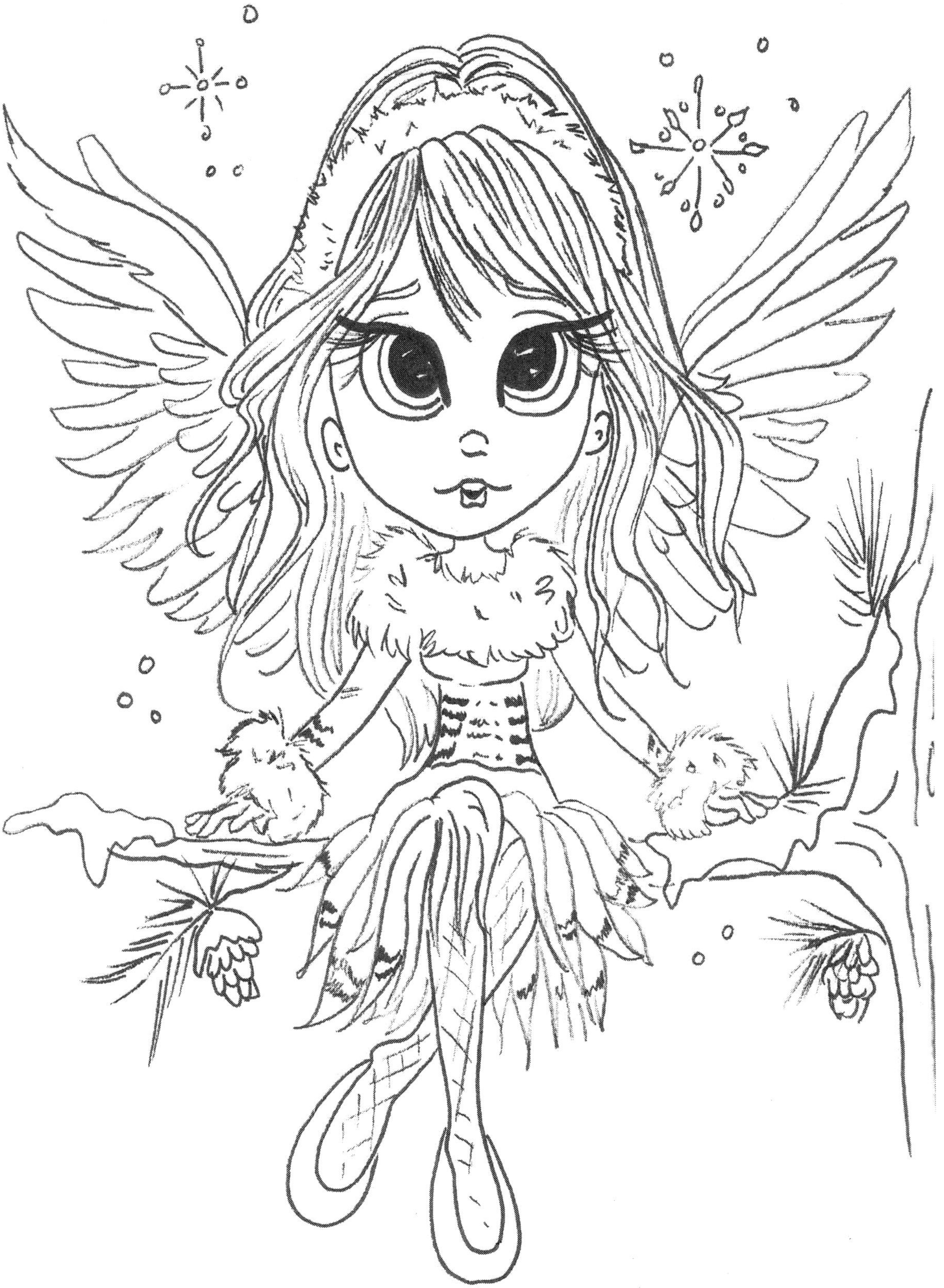

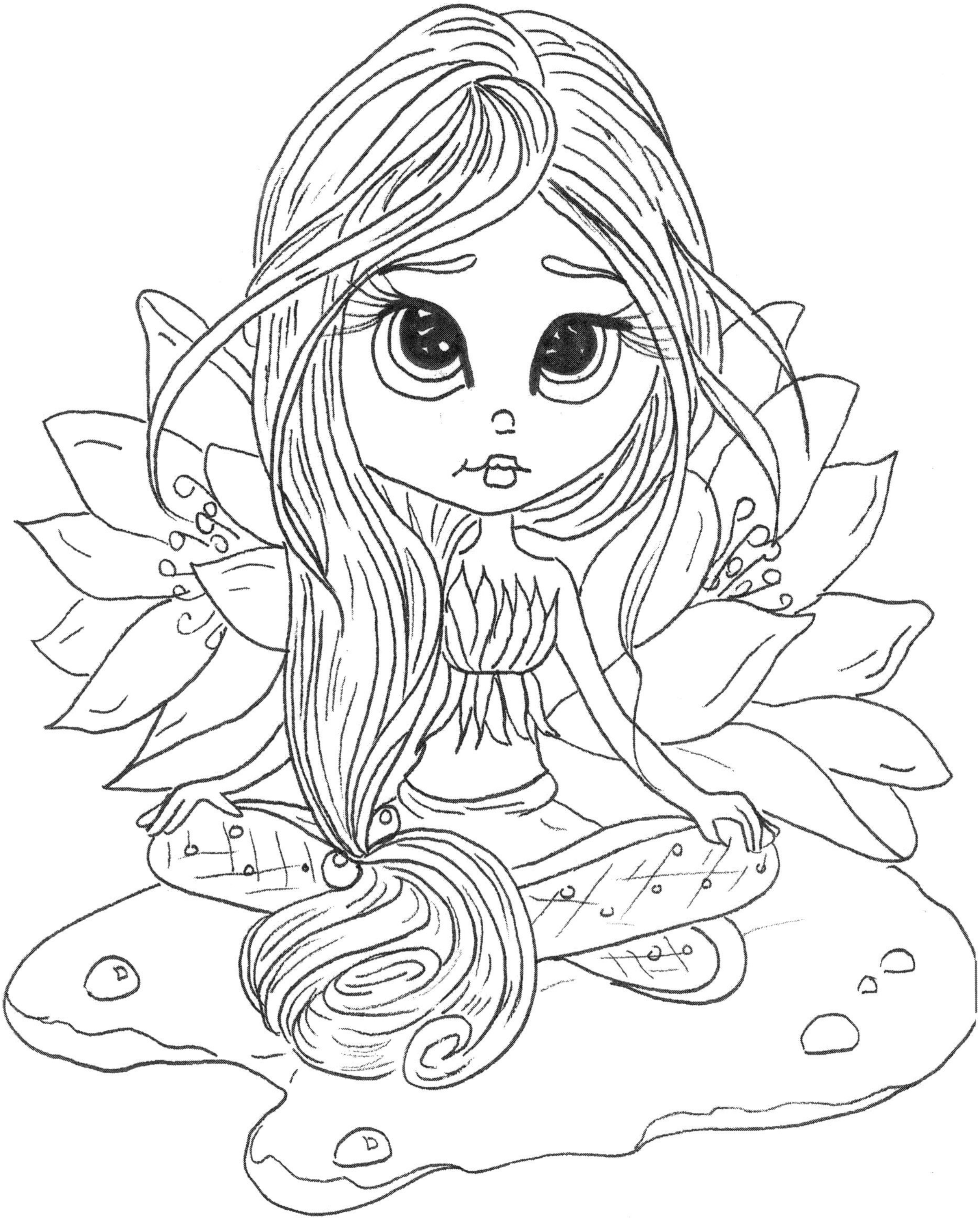

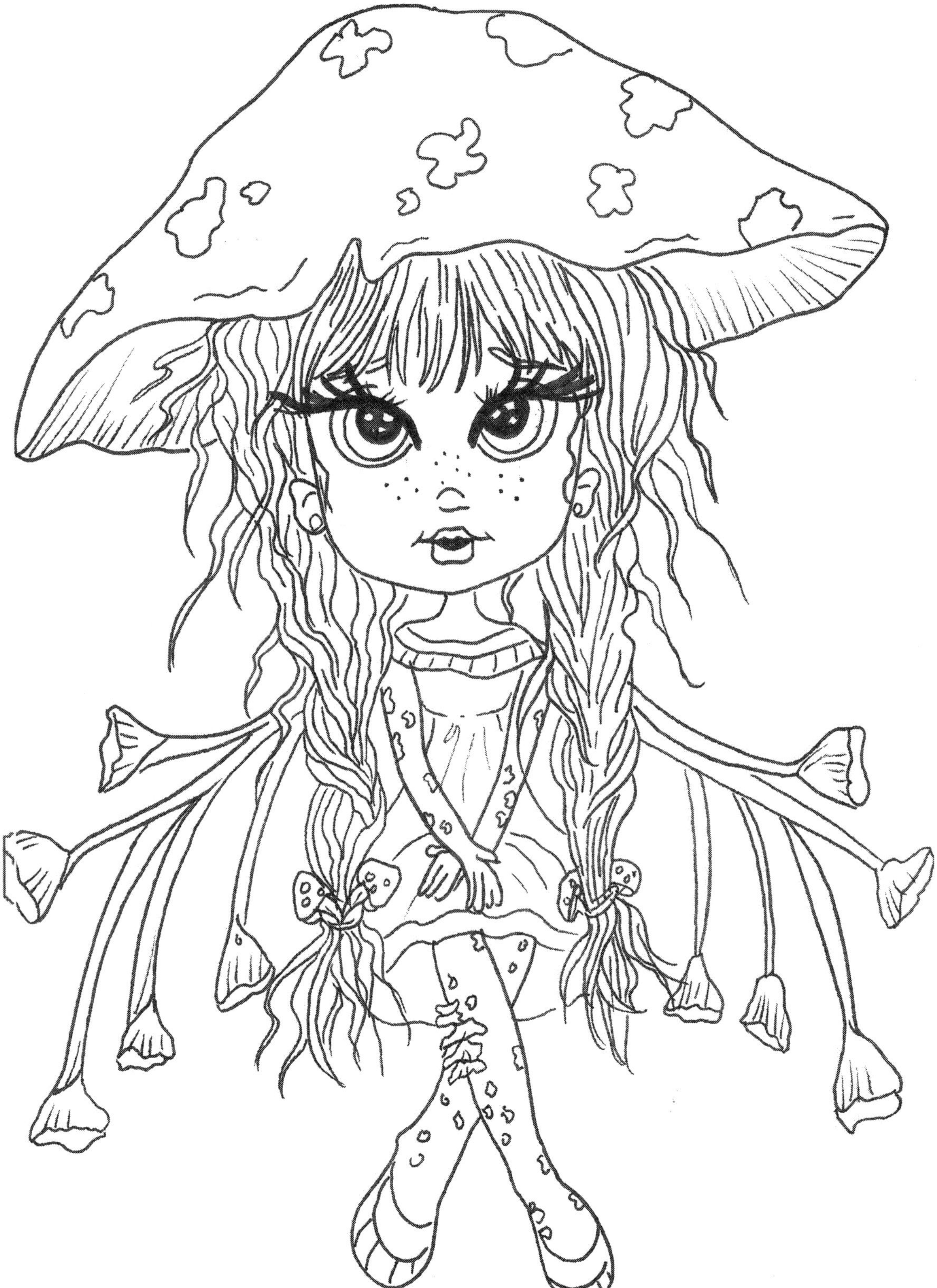

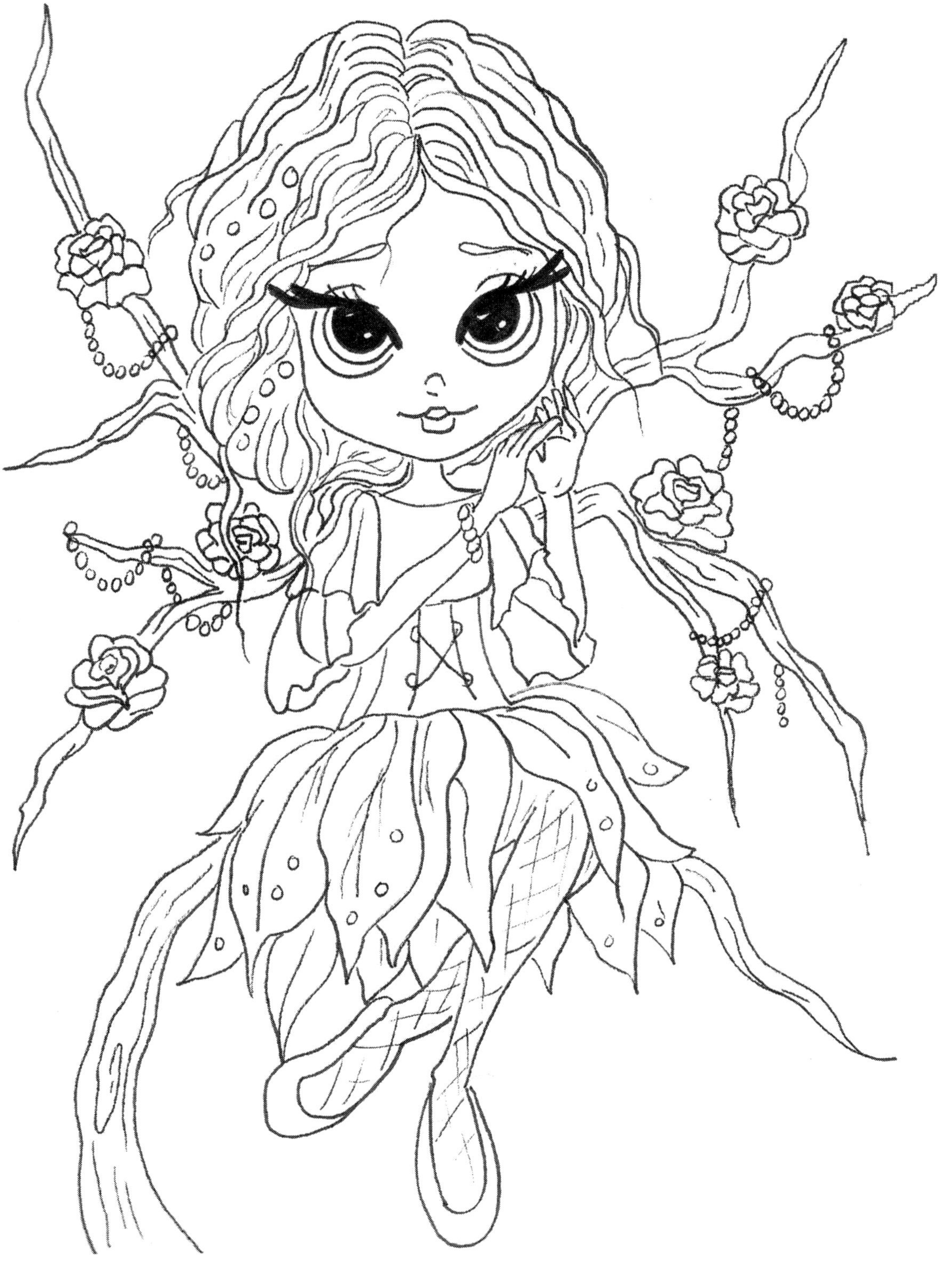

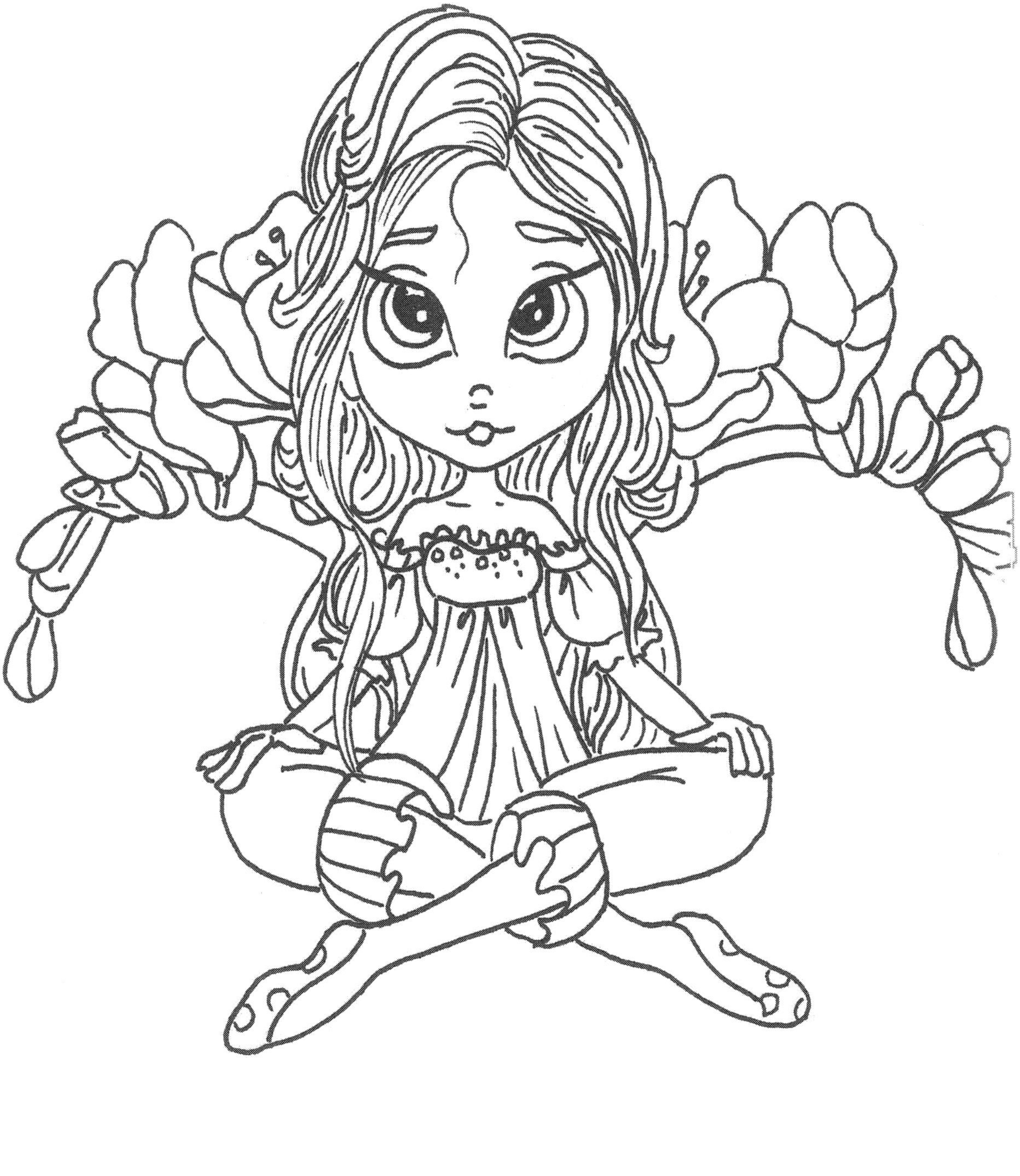

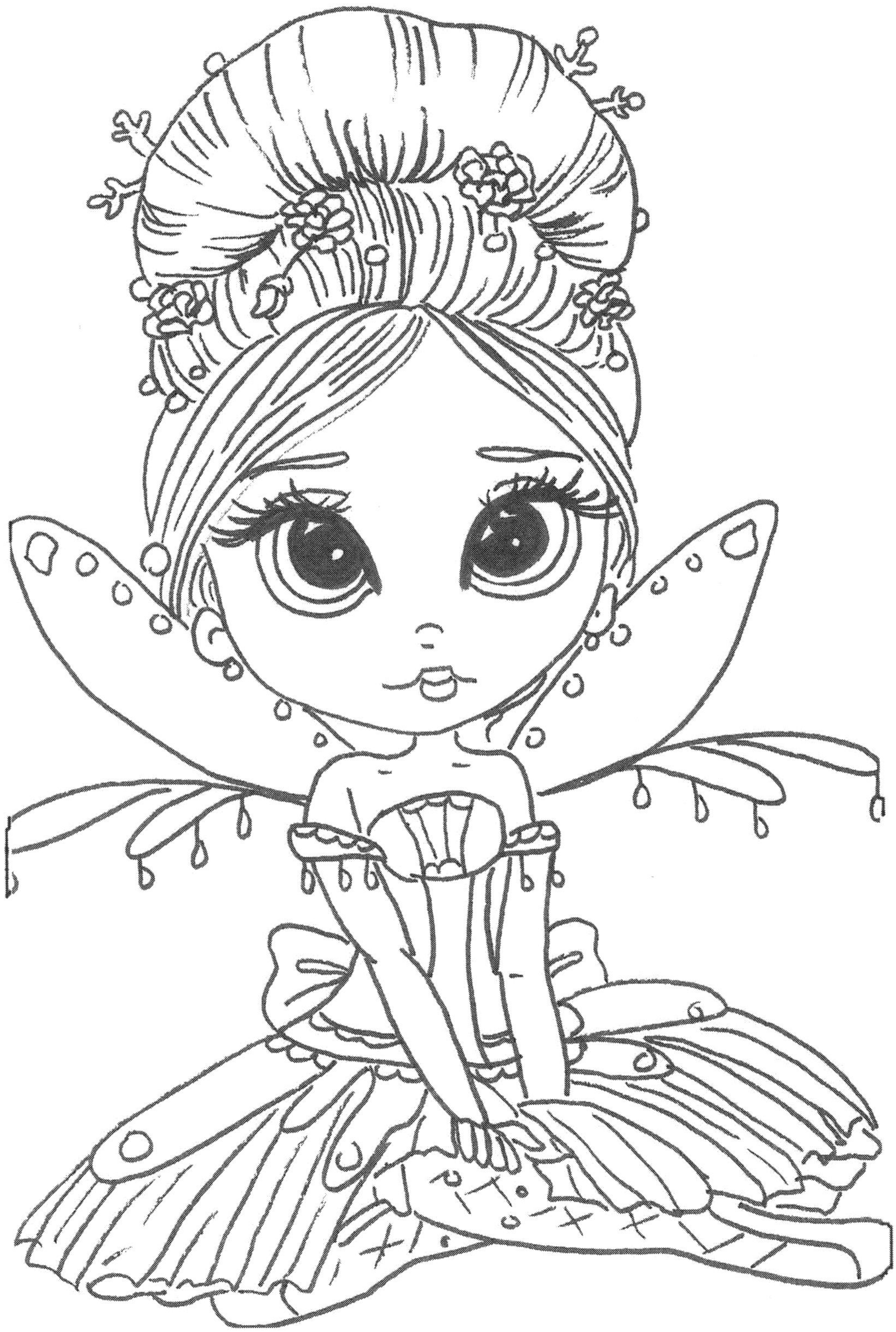

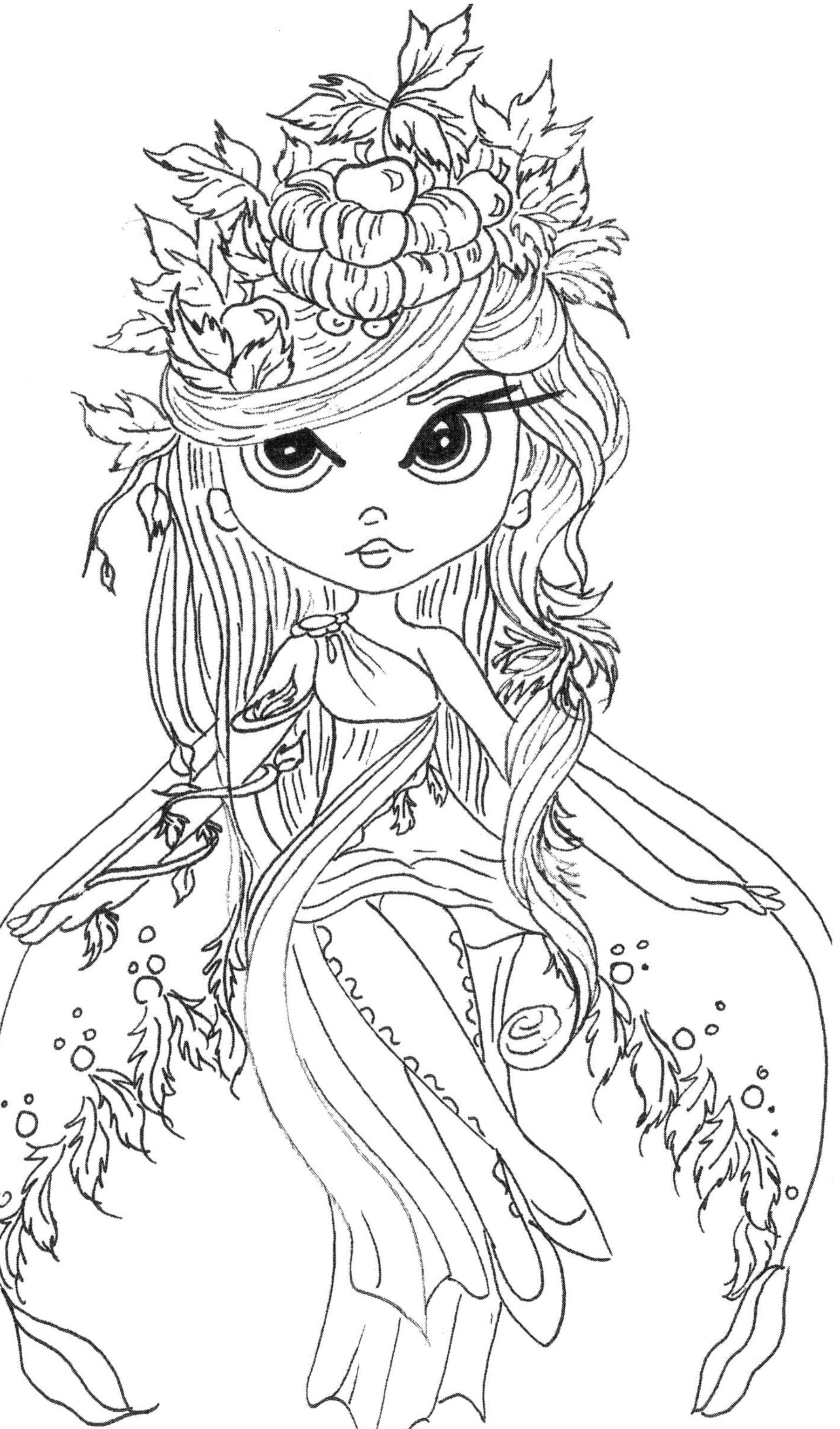

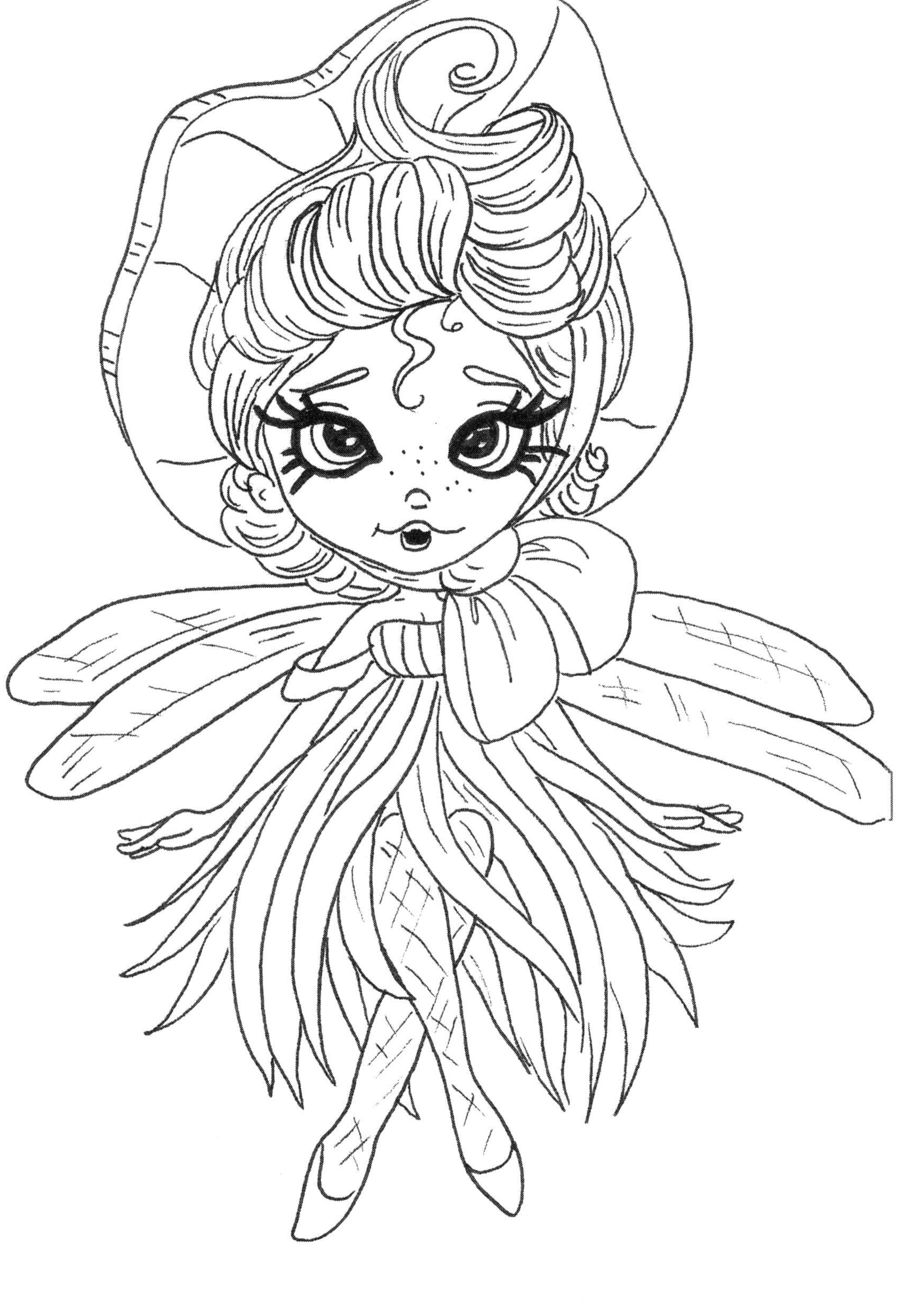

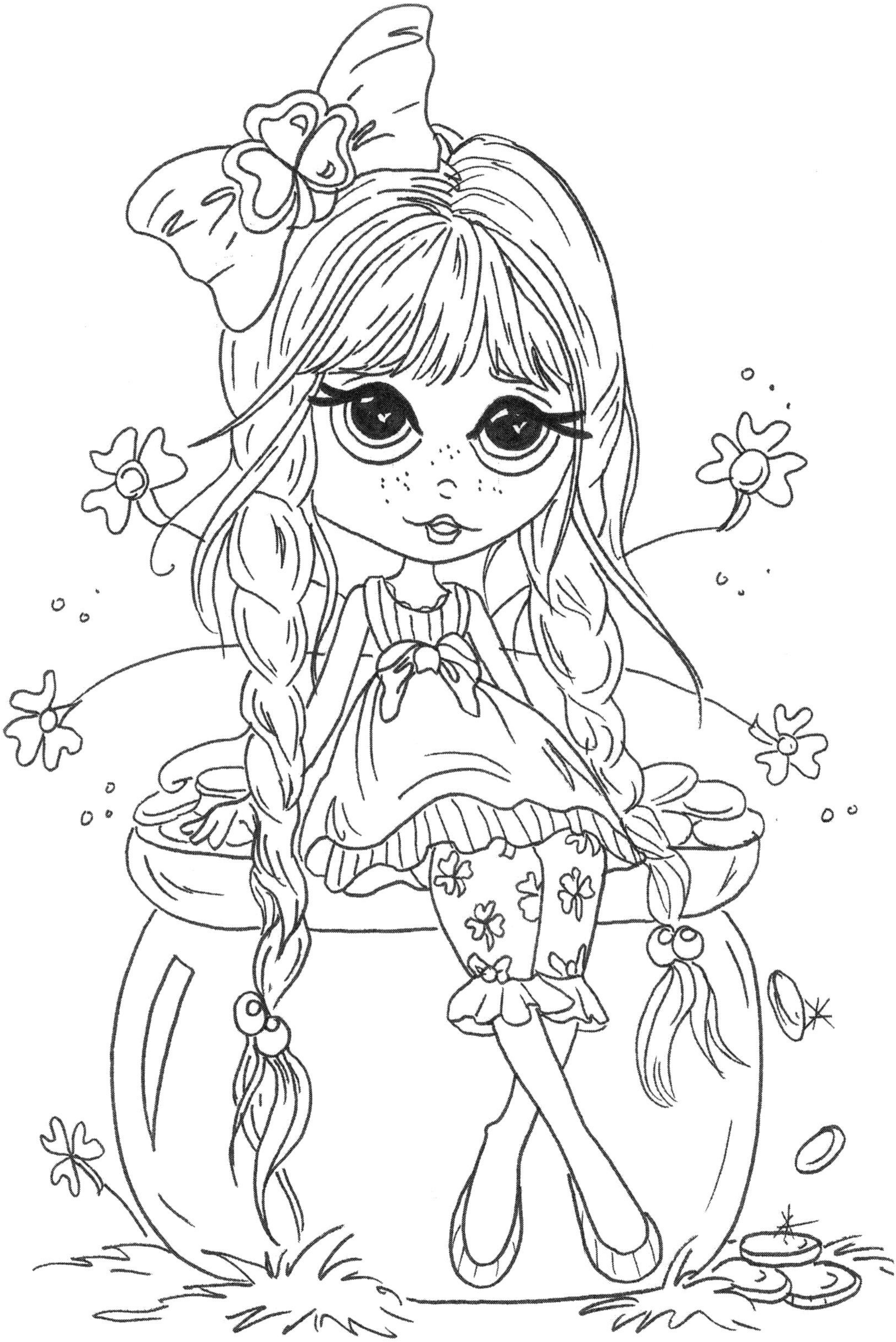

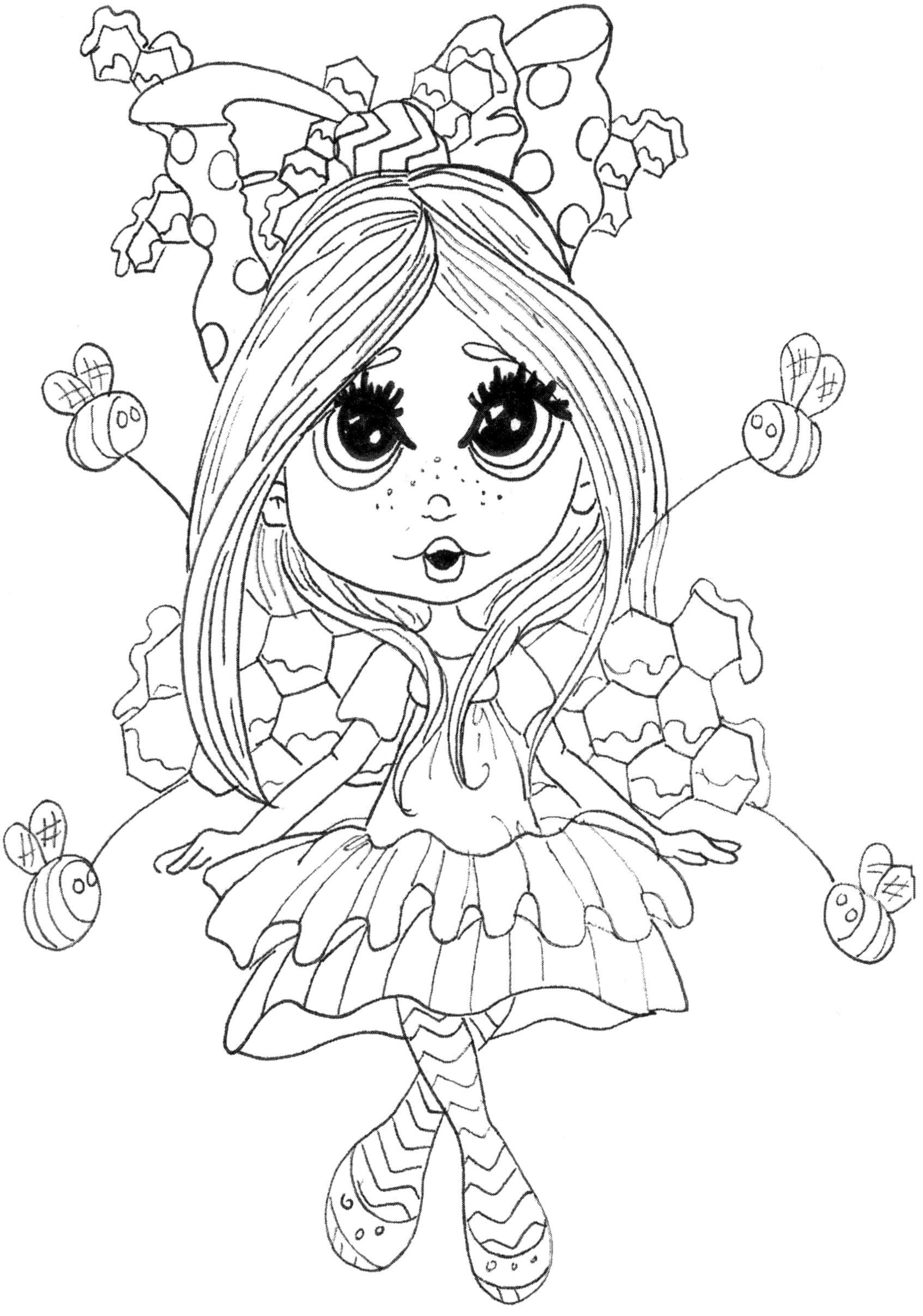

66287400R00049

Made in the USA
Middletown, DE
09 March 2018